# High-Stakes Antitrust

# High-Stakes Antitrust
## The Last Hurrah?

Robert W. Hahn
*Editor*

AEI-BROOKINGS JOINT CENTER
FOR REGULATORY STUDIES
*Washington, D.C.*

*High Stakes Antitrust* may be ordered from:
Brookings Institution Press
1775 Massachusetts Avenue, N.W.
Washington, D.C. 20036
Tel.: (800) 275-1447 or (202) 797-2960
Fax: (202) 797-6004
*www.brookings.edu*

*Library of Congress Cataloging-in-Publication data*
High-stakes antitrust : the last hurrah? / Robert W. Hahn, editor.
    p.    cm.
Includes bibliographical references and index.
    ISBN 0-8157-3396-8 (cloth : alk. paper) —
    ISBN 0-8157-3395-X (pbk. : alk. paper)
    1.  Antitrust law—United States.  I. Hahn, Robert William.  II.
AEI-Brookings Joint Center for Regulatory Studies. III. Title.
    KF1649.A2H54 2003
    343.73'0721—dc22                                          2003015789

9 8 7 6 5 4 3 2 1

The paper used in this publication meets minimum requirements of the American National Standard for Information Sciences—Permanence of Paper for Printed Library Materials: ANSI Z39.48-1992.

Typeset in Adobe Garamond

Composition by R. Lynn Rivenbark
Macon, Georgia

Printed by R. R. Donnelley
Harrisonburg, Virginia

# Contents

# Foreword

After almost two decades in which antitrust policy had veered sharply toward less-is-more, the rules changed in the late 1990s. The U.S. Department of Justice mounted challenges to the practices of successful service enterprises in payment cards, airlines, and software.

All three antitrust suits involved industries in which networks played a significant role. Do interventions in these network industries signal a return to an era in which Washington second-guesses market outcomes, rather than simply setting ground rules for competition and allowing markets to respond on their own?

This collection of essays provides a state-of-the-art analysis of high-stakes antitrust issues raised over the past decade. It is the result of an AEI-Brookings Joint Center for Regulatory Studies conference held on October 3, 2002.

The scholars who participated reflected diverse points of view. While each of the four panelists agreed to two basic facts—first, that the Department of Justice's approach to antitrust in the 1990s was aggressive and, second, that the impact of the landmark cases filed in that decade will be felt for many years to come—agreement mostly ends there. Two of the panelists argued that the department had lost its way, albeit for different reasons. The other two panelists argued that while the Justice Department missed some opportunities and made some missteps, its aggressive stance was largely justified by changing technology and market conditions.

This volume is one in a series of books commissioned by the AEI-Brookings Joint Center for Regulatory Studies to contribute to the continuing debate over antitrust. The Joint Center builds on the expertise of both sponsoring institutions on regulatory issues. The series addresses several fundamental issues in antitrust and regulation, including the design of effective reforms, the impact of proposed reforms on the public, and the political and institutional forces that affect reform. We hope that these publications will help illuminate many of the complex issues involved in designing and implementing regulation and regulatory reforms at all levels of government.

The views expressed here are those of the authors and should not be attributed to the trustees, officers, or staff members of the American Enterprise Institute or the Brookings Institution.

ROBERT W. HAHN
*Executive Director*
ROBERT E. LITAN
*Director*
*AEI-Brookings Joint Center for Regulatory Studies*

ROBERT W. HAHN

# 1 | *Introduction*

A fter almost two decades in which antitrust policy
veered sharply toward the philosophy that less is
more, the policy changed in the late 1990s when the U.S. Department of
Justice mounted challenges to the practices of successful service enterprises
dealing in software (Microsoft), consumer payment cards (Visa and
MasterCard), and air travel (American Airlines).

All three antitrust suits involved industries in which networks were
crucial. Microsoft supports a network of hardware manufacturers, personal
computer vendors, computer users, and software developers that depend
on the company's Windows operating system. Visa and MasterCard have
created vast networks of merchants who accept credit, charge, and debit
cards that are issued to consumers by thousands of financial institutions.
American Airlines operates an air carrier network connecting hundreds of
cities worldwide.

Do challenges to the practices of these network industries signal a
return to an era in which Washington second-guessed market outcomes
instead of simply setting ground rules for competition and allowing markets to respond on their own? Or were antitrust activities of the later Clinton years an aberration—a last hurrah for hard-line trustbusting? In October 2002 the AEI-Brookings Joint Center for Regulatory Studies invited
experts with a variety of perspectives on those questions to discuss them

and to assess the future of antitrust policy. This book presents a compendium of their thinking.

The panelists agreed on two basic facts: that the approach of the Department of Justice to enforcement of antitrust legislation in the late 1990s was aggressive and that the impact of the cases filed then will be felt for many years to come. Agreement, for the most part, ended there. Two of the panelists argued, albeit for different reasons, that the Justice Department had lost its way. The other two argued that while the department missed some opportunities and made some missteps, its aggressive stance was largely justified by changing technology and market conditions.

This introduction offers a summary of the four viewpoints, noting both differences and common themes. Lawrence J. White, of the Stern School of Business at New York University, presents the most comprehensive discussion of Clinton-era antitrust policy, so I begin with his chapter. Robert Bork, with the American Enterprise Institute, is narrower in focus, but he agrees with White that the Clinton administration's antitrust policy was based on sound law and economic theory. The final two chapters take a very different stance, arguing that the antitrust policy of the Clinton administration was ill conceived. Howard H. Chang, David S. Evans (both with NERA Economic Consulting), and Richard Schmalensee (at the Massachusetts Institute of Technology) argue that the Justice Department ignored consumer harm as a criterion for pursuing two of the three high-stakes suits of the 1990s. George L. Priest, at the Yale Law School, agrees, but he contends that the lack of focus on consumers stemmed from a fundamental misunderstanding of network industries.

In "Antitrust Activities during the Clinton Administration: An Assessment," Lawrence White offers a relatively sanguine assessment of antitrust actions during the 1990s. In his review, covering far more than just the *Microsoft*, *Visa/MasterCard*, and *American Airlines* cases, he concedes that the decade did bring a "new activism" to antitrust enforcement efforts. But White maintains that continuity remained strong, that the basic approach of earlier regimes was not changed. For example, the Justice Department stood by the *Horizontal Merger Guidelines* promulgated in the 1980s.[1] And despite the wave of mergers in the late 1990s, neither the Justice Department nor the Federal Trade Commission succumbed to what he labels "populist temptations" to block conglomerate mergers.

1. U.S. Department of Justice and Federal Trade Commission (1992).

To put antitrust enforcement during the decade into perspective, White refers to a variety of cases. With regard to *Microsoft*, he describes the software maker as a dominant firm operating in a market in which entry is difficult and contends that the company went out of its way to raise its rivals' costs and to increase its market power.[2] White argues that while the Justice Department's challenge of Microsoft was not entirely coherent, it was justified. Similarly, the debates about overlapping governance of the payment card system and of card issuance in *Visa/MasterCard* were worth raising and the case itself worth pursuing.

White argues that the case against American Airlines was not as clear cut as either *Microsoft* or *Visa/MasterCard* but the situation still justified the intervention. In the more than two decades following airline deregulation, he observes, few new carriers have been able to survive competition from the large incumbent airlines. Certainly, the hub-and-spoke design of the incumbents is an effective means for taking advantage of network economies. But White argues that the incumbents abused their market position by expanding the frequency of flights in response to their rivals' entry, even as they matched their fares.

White acknowledges that it is difficult to differentiate aggressive competition from predatory behavior, especially when nonprice predation, such as an increase in passenger capacity, is at issue. Nonetheless, it is important to try to make the distinction in situations that include a dominant firm, strong market concentration, and difficult market entry—and where it is realistic to expect that losses from predatory behavior can be recouped. American Airlines fit those criteria, White says; therefore, despite the fact that the government lost, the suit was justified and pushed predation theory forward.

After discussing these three, White touches on other cases brought during the latter half of the 1990s. *Intel* and *Dentsply* focused on the problems of raising rivals' costs; *Toys "R" Us* came to grips with important issues of vertical restraints on trade; *Staples*, *MCI WorldCom–Sprint*, and *Heinz–Beech-Nut* raised significant merger issues, including the question of when company promises of postmerger efficiencies should outweigh concerns over postmerger industry concentration. Whether the government won or lost, he argues, the pursuit of those cases advanced antitrust jurisprudence.

2. Full citations to the cases mentioned here appear in the various chapters.

White does contend, however, that the antitrust agencies made some missteps and missed some opportunities altogether during the 1990s. For example, he argues that the Federal Trade Commission miscalculated when it chose not to present empirical evidence in *California Dental*, which led the court of appeals to recommend that the case be dropped. Regarding missed opportunities, he would have liked either the FTC or the Justice Department to challenge the Bell Atlantic–NYNEX merger on grounds that the match would eliminate potential competition. Moreover, he argues that the failure to develop vertical-restraint guidelines left a significant hole in antitrust policy.

Taken as whole, White concludes, the antitrust enforcers of the late 1990s followed in the footsteps of their predecessors. Several cases filed during that time were controversial, but they had a "solid analytical foundation." In the end, he says, the Clinton antitrust legacy is a mix of important initiatives leavened with some missed opportunities.

Robert Bork, whose chapter, "High-Stakes Antitrust: The Last Hurrah?," focuses on the three high-profile cases, agrees with White concerning the overall direction of Clinton antitrust policy. Bork comments that although the current Bush administration has "less appetite" for path-breaking antitrust suits than its predecessor, enthusiasm for enforcement of antitrust law has always tended to cycle. High-stakes antitrust actions are sure to return. Bork also agrees that of the prominent cases of the 1990s, *Microsoft* and *Visa/MasterCard* were clearly justified, pointing out that both involved organizations with market power whose executives viewed network effects as insufficient protection for their monopoly status.

*Microsoft*, Bork argues, was one of the few cases in which a court of appeals sitting en banc unanimously upheld a finding of predation by a monopolist. He presents several examples of Microsoft's predatory behavior, defining predation as employing tactics other than efficiency to eliminate competitors. Although he acknowledges that internal company communications can be very misleading, couched as they often are in the language of war, he nonetheless argues that Microsoft's e-mails exposed its predatory intent. When it became apparent to the company that network effects and the "applications barrier to entry" were insufficient to protect its monopoly profits, it turned to a predatory campaign. The e-mails laid out the means by which it would attack its rivals, and the company's actions matched those plans.[3]

3. For two other views on this case see Evans and others (2000).

In Bork's view it is unfortunate that the negotiated *Microsoft* settlement did not capitalize on the government's resounding victory in the courts. The consent decree, he observes, did not even prohibit the behavior the district court and the en banc court of appeals held illegal. Of most concern is the lack of a prohibition on "commingling" the software code for the Windows operating system with other software codes, such as that for Microsoft's Internet Explorer browser.

*Visa/MasterCard,* Bork contends, was similar to *Microsoft* in that it involved the abuse of monopoly power. He argues, moreover, that the government's case was "if not quite a slam dunk, close to it." The two cooperatives had a selective view of competition. They deemed American Express and Discover to be direct competitors that had to be excluded from Visa and MasterCard's systems but allowed member banks to issue one another's cards—and allowed one member, Citibank, to issue Diners Club cards as well. The result of Visa and MasterCard's card issuance rules was thus to narrow consumers' choice in credit and charge cards and to limit new offerings in debit and multifunction, chip-enabled "smart" cards.

As for the two cooperatives' counterargument that opening the system to American Express would give that company the opportunity to skim off the best banks, Bork asserts that both Visa and MasterCard already do that themselves, that indeed such "cherry-picking" is what competition is about. Thus he agrees with the district court decision that the bank associations' card-issuing rules were in violation of section 1 of the Sherman Anti-Trust Act.

In contrast, Bork contends that the government's case against American Airlines was off target. Here, he distances himself from White, arguing that the Justice Department's lack of a clear remedy emphasizes the faulty logic behind the case. Although this action, like *Microsoft* and *Visa/MasterCard,* involved network industries, unlike computer operating systems and payment cards, networks in the airline industry facilitate competition. Multiple networks currently exist and compete against each other, Bork contends, and competition is strong among hubs and among airlines. He points out that American never priced below the low-cost carrier entrants; indeed, at the low prices met by American, demand was sure to be greater. Thus the airline's fares and flight expansions on the contested routes fall under the defense of "meeting competition," which should apply to the Sherman Act as well as to the Robinson-Patman Act.

If lowering prices to competitors' levels and increasing output were anticompetitive, what remedy could the courts reasonably impose? Should

American have to maintain its relatively high prices and relatively less frequent flights in the face of competition? If not, should the courts put themselves in the position of dictating American's legal minimum fares, which would be somewhere between the old American price and the low-cost carriers' price? Bork argues that because none of these options makes economic or legal sense, they expose the shaky foundation of the government's case against the airline.

In "Has the Consumer Harm Standard Lost Its Teeth?" Howard Chang, David Evans, and Richard Schmalensee argue that the foundations for the government's cases against both Microsoft and Visa/MasterCard were shaky as well. They point to a lack of focus on consumers in the Justice Department's antitrust efforts during the 1990s. In particular, they contend that the Clinton Justice Department relied on the assumption that harm to competitors automatically led to harm to consumers. In both *Microsoft* and *Visa/MasterCard*, as well as in *Intel*, a contemporary case that was settled before going to trial, the government confounded two distinct concepts. Harm to a competitor does not inevitably imply harm to the competitive process and thus harm to consumers, the prevention of which is the ultimate goal of antitrust laws. To link the two concepts, the Department of Justice should have presented direct evidence that the challenged practices had raised prices, lowered output, reduced quality, or otherwise harmed consumers.

At the heart of any standard of consumer harm adopted by the courts is the tension between the risk of being too lenient and the risk of being too strict. If a standard is too lenient, companies come to believe that they can behave anticompetitively without risk of government intervention. If a standard is too strict, courts will condemn practices that help consumers, undermining competition instead of spurring it. Because the courts cannot eliminate both risks at once, the goal is to set the standard to minimize the expected costs of the inevitable errors. The authors contend that the consumer harm standard espoused by the Clinton Justice Department risked discouraging procompetitive practices. Rather than demonstrating actual or likely consumer harm, the government presented evidence that competitors were harmed and that those competitors were important to the industry. The department, they point out, did not show that harm to those important competitors actually harmed the competitive process and thereby harmed consumers.[4]

---

4. Bork challenges the contention that the government must provide proof of harm to consumers. He argues instead that consumer harm can be inferred from "certain forms of exclusionary market

In *Microsoft* the Justice Department claimed that Netscape had the potential to create competition for Microsoft's Windows platform and that Microsoft's actions undermined Netscape's potential to challenge Windows. Determining whether Netscape was in fact a nascent threat is not easy, but the authors argue that the government could have attempted to buttress its case with empirical analysis. For example, did the actions Microsoft took that were deemed illegal by the appeals court in fact reduce Netscape's share of the market for Internet browsers below the threshold necessary to form an alternative platform to Windows?

Chang, Evans, and Schmalensee go on to say that one of Microsoft's economic experts did compare Netscape browser use among a control group of Internet users whose choice of browsers was not likely to be affected by the anticompetitive acts and a group of users whose browser choice could have been affected by those acts. Microsoft's expert found an insignificant difference between the two groups, implying that the company's actions did not play an important part in reducing Netscape's browser share. Certainly experts can disagree on the proper way of measuring harm, and the authors do not advocate one particular set of tests. Rather, they argue that the Justice Department never engaged in that debate; it simply did not present evidence that Microsoft undermined competition or harmed consumers.

In *Visa/MasterCard*, the authors observe, the government never attempted to determine the extent to which competitors—American Express and Discover—were harmed by Visa's and MasterCard's refusal to let their network members join competing systems. Nor did the government try to measure the extent to which the alleged harm to American Express and Discover generally affected competition in payment cards. As with *Microsoft*, the authors contend that those issues could have been addressed empirically. For example, the government could have used quantitative analysis to back its claim that additional issuers lead to increased card issuance. It also could have assessed whether additional issuance had benefited consumers in the past through lower prices or higher quality.

---

behavior." Once the government raised the possibility of consumer harm through inference, defendants had the burden of proof to show that their actions resulted in efficiencies. Chang, Evans, and Schmalensee counter these comments by arguing that, while direct proof is not always possible, the "quick look" standard Bork advocates is inadequate. At a minimum, the inference of consumer harm through harm to a competitor should be backed by evidence that the competitor suffered injury significant enough to limit its effectiveness. Only after consumer harm has been established should the court turn to the impact on economic efficiency.

In the opinion of Chang, Evans, and Schmalensee, an error-cost analysis suggests that a strong standard for consumer harm would reduce the cost of a false conviction while keeping the cost of a false acquittal relatively low. They argue that the Department of Justice should have been more rigorous in presenting proof of consumer harm. It remains to be seen whether other circuit courts and eventually the Supreme Court will reject the Clinton Justice Department's lax approach.

Also seizing on the extent of consumer harm, George Priest argues in "The Government's Flawed Efforts to Apply Modern Antitrust Law to Network Industries" that the central problem in the Clinton Justice Department's approach to enforcement of antitrust law was its failure to explain how competition between networks would benefit consumers. Priest posits that the department failed in this effort because it did not possess a coherent theory of how networks should best be organized. It never showed that introducing additional competition at the network level would benefit consumers. Moreover, the department's arguments in the three prominent cases were inconsistent, and no attempt was made to synthesize an overarching argument for how antitrust laws should apply to networks.

Priest contends that in *Microsoft*, the government did not develop a theory of how a market with multiple competing operating systems would function to the benefit of consumers or even be able to sustain itself. Nor did the government explain why, if substantial benefits could have been realized from multiple systems, such competition had not developed through market forces. Priest points out that the Justice Department acknowledged that Microsoft had earned its operating system dominance on the merits of the system—that is, the department never claimed that Microsoft had broken the law in establishing its monopoly.

Bear in mind, Priest comments, that markets for operating systems, like those for other network products, are winner-take-most markets. Typically, competition is *for* the market, not *within* the market. Thus, if no illegal acts were committed in gaining the operating system monopoly, the dominance reflects the work of market forces—the network benefits arising from standardizing operating systems and from developing scores of applications compatible with that system. Therefore, the government's case was predicated on a contradiction.

Priest contends that the Justice Department made similar mistakes in its suit against Visa and MasterCard. On one hand it argued that a bank sitting on the board of one of the cooperatives should be precluded from sitting on the board of the other, that the governance structures of the two associations should be completely separate so as to foster competition. On the other hand it argued that it was anticompetitive for Visa and Master-Card to prevent their members from issuing American Express and Discover cards. That is, at the level of the individual member the systems should not be separate—indeed, that members should merge the card issuance networks by offering as many brands as possible. These two ambitions are internally inconsistent, Priest observes, and moreover the claim that member exclusion rules are anticompetitive is inconsistent with the department's arguments in *Microsoft*. The department attempted to create new, separate networks in *Microsoft* but asked the court to force the merger of existing competing networks in *Visa/MasterCard*.

In *American Airlines* Priest maintains that the government's case was lacking for a different reason. There the Justice Department chose to ignore the network character of the airline industry. Rather than acknowledge that American's passenger service operated in a network of routes, it limited its focus to routes between selected cities also served by low-cost carriers. It claimed that American set predatory prices and unfairly increased capacity on these routes in response to competition. But Priest notes that the allegedly predatory prices were identical to fares charged by the low-cost carriers, and it is difficult to see how improving service is anticompetitive. When American's costs are calculated in a way that accounts for running a network, as opposed to operating a handful of disjointed routes, the case for predatory pricing collapses.

According to Priest, the government's arguments in these three cases did not advance the application of antitrust laws in an evolving economy. At best the Justice Department ignored the implications of network industries; at worst its arguments were inconsistent and contradictory, lacking a coherent theory of how competition among networks benefits consumers.

The four viewpoints represented in this book can be reduced to two basic positions. White and Bork largely support the government's antitrust efforts in the late 1990s. Although they recognize some mistakes on the part of the Justice Department and Federal Trade Commission, they nonetheless believe that the antitrust arguments the government put forth were well grounded in legal and economic theory. Chang and his colleagues and Priest, however, contend that the antitrust enforcement was based on faulty economic logic and did little to advance antitrust jurisprudence. In particular, the government lost sight of the driving force behind antitrust enforcement: harm to consumers.

The two-viewpoint description, though, glosses over some important differences: White and Bork disagree about *American Airlines* and Chang and colleagues and Priest disagree about the primary cause of the Justice Department's missteps. Indeed, each chapter makes different arguments stemming from different vantage points. White holds that despite the government's loss, *American Airlines* was important because it advanced the thinking on what constitutes predation. Bork disagrees, stating that vague worries about competition with low-cost carriers are no substitute for well-thought-out economic theory. On this point, at least, Priest agrees with Bork. Priest argues that the government's lack of understanding about network industries in general led to a confused attack on several companies operating in those industries. Chang, Evans, and Schmalensee do not even discuss *American Airlines;* they argue instead that the government's failures in antitrust enforcement during the 1990s stem not from a poor understanding of networks, but from a poor evidentiary standard for proving consumer harm.

Had AEI and Brookings invited additional observers to contribute to the debate, it is likely there would have been still more viewpoints. But regardless of the variety, one thing is clear: given the far-reaching nature of the major antitrust cases brought under the Clinton administration, its antitrust legacy is likely to be felt for quite some time.

## References

Evans, David S., and others. 2000. *Did Microsoft Harm Consumers? Two Opposing Views.* AEI–Brookings Joint Center for Regulatory Studies.

U.S. Department of Justice and Federal Trade Commission. 1997. "Horizontal Merger Guidelines." 57 *Federal Register* 41, 552 (1992), revised 4 *Trade Register Ep (CCH)*, para. 13,104 (April 8).

LAWRENCE J. WHITE

# 2 | *Antitrust Activities during the Clinton Administration*

A ny assessment of the antitrust record of a presiden-
tial administration must necessarily involve sub-
jective judgments about the merits of cases brought and not brought as
well as about the broad sweep of policy and perspective. This chapter will
be no exception.[1]

Let us begin with some historical perspective on events ten years ago.
The Clinton administration took office in early 1993 after twelve years of
Republican control of the White House. Among the Democratic complaints about those dozen years of control was that the Antitrust Division of
the U.S. Department of Justice and the Federal Trade Commission had
been lax in antitrust enforcement. Too many mergers had been permitted,
allowing market concentration to rise too high in too many industries; the
airlines were a notable example.[2] A second complaint was that enforcement

Thanks are due to Jonathan Baker, David Balto, Timothy Brennan, Timothy Bresnahan, Stephen
Calkins, Harry First, Robert Hahn, Stephen Houck, Anjela Kniazeva, and Douglas Melamed for comments on an earlier draft.

1. For other retrospectives see Balto (1999); Litan and Shapiro (2002); Pitofsky (2002a, 2002b).

2. The airlines were, however, also an ambiguous example. The formal antitrust enforcer, the
Department of Justice, had opposed two high-profile airline mergers in the 1980s: Northwest-Republic
and TWA-Ozark. However, unlike most mergers, as a consequence of the Airline Deregulation Act of
1978 (passed by a Democratic Congress and signed by a Democratic president), authority for ultimate
approval of airline mergers rested with the Department of Transportation, which had approved them

of prohibitions on vertical restraints (such as tying, exclusive dealing, and refusals to deal) and on predatory behavior was inadequate. The administration promised a new activism in antitrust policy and enforcement.

And there was a new activism. Cases were brought that probably would not have been initiated during the previous regimes. But the elements of continuity were strong as well.[3] There certainly was no revolutionary overturning of major directions of the previous regimes, and there was no return to the populism and enthusiasm for protecting small business that had sometimes colored antitrust policy before the 1980s.

## A Methodological Issue

One important methodological issue should be addressed at the beginning: how to judge the stringency (or laxness) of antitrust enforcement. Such judgments cannot be made on the basis solely of numbers of cases initiated or litigated.[4] This important point is readily apparent in the context of merger enforcement.[5] Regardless of the legal standards that are being enforced, if the standards themselves are unchanging, are clearly known to the private bar, and there are no ambiguities, no potentially illegal mergers would ever be proposed. An illegal merger would surely be rejected by enforcers, the potential partners would be wasting their time, and knowledgeable legal counsel would prevent their going forward. And with no illegal mergers ever proposed, there would be no enforcement actions.[6] An immediate implication is that for a given level of enforcement *effort*, the

---

over the Justice Department's objections. The law has since been changed to give the Justice Department standard Clayton Act authority with respect to airline mergers.

3. One important element of continuity was the prominent use of economics and economists in antitrust litigation. For a discussion see Kwoka and White (1999, 2004a). For a longer view concerning the rise of economics at the Justice Department and the Federal Trade Commission see Eisner (1991); Kwoka and White (1989, 1994).

4. Discussions of antitrust policy that include case counts are common. For a recent discussion see Litan and Shapiro (2002); for an older discussion see Eisner (1991).

5. In addition to their case counts, Litan and Shapiro (2002) also acknowledge that certainty with respect to merger standards can reduce litigation.

6. As a further elaboration on the pattern of merger enforcement actions, until the passage of the Hart-Scott-Rodino (HSR) amendments to the Clayton Act in 1976, the enforcement agencies sometimes found out about mergers late and had to scramble to sue and seek a preliminary injunction to forestall those that were deemed potentially anticompetitive—and then negotiate to determine if a divestiture could solve the antitrust problem. With Hart-Scott-Rodino prenotification procedures in place a "fix it first" policy was far more feasible, and the number of legal challenges diminished.

number of enforcement *actions* (and litigation generally) will be related to the extent of uncertainties and ambiguities about legal outcomes perceived by defendants.[7]

Of course, an outcome of no enforcement actions could also result from lack of enforcement effort. But this second means of achieving no enforcement actions highlights the ambiguity of the relevance of counting the number of enforcement actions and of any change in the number of actions during a given time. If the number is low, the reason could be lax enforcement or it could be clear legal standards and a reputation for vigorous enforcement.[8] Similarly, if enforcement actions decrease from one year to the next, the reason could be fewer enforcement efforts or greater clarity of the legal standards.

Accordingly, in the absence of more information, counts of legal actions by themselves ought not to carry much weight. Instead, to ascertain the stringency of enforcement, one must discern the nature (or the "line") of the legal standards (what behavior is challenged; what behavior is unchallenged) and the consistency with which those standards are enforced.

To drive this point home, consider the assumptions that would justify using numbers of enforcement actions as indicators of enforcement vigor. Suppose that there is a constant background flow of violations that is invariant to the amount of enforcement effort (or the uncertainty of enforcement). If that is so, then enforcement involves scooping into the flow. More enforcement effort will result in more scoops and thus more enforcement actions, and the number of actions can be used as an indicator of the vigor of the effort. But this notion of a constant background flow of crimes is inconsistent with the idea of deterrence—that enforcement can deter crimes and thus affect the flow.[9] Consequently, anyone who believes in deterrence ought not to believe in a constant-flow model and should not place great weight on counts of enforcement actions as indicators of enforcement vigor or stringency.[10]

---

7. Baxter (1980); Priest and Klein (1984); Salop and White (1986, 1988); White (1988).

8. This clarity might be due to a large number of enforcement actions in earlier periods, the outcomes of which helped clarify the legal standard and create the reputation of tough enforcement.

9. For illustration, if there are no police patrolling a neighborhood, there will be no arrests; but if the police blanket a neighborhood so thoroughly that criminals are deterred, there will also be no arrests.

10. There may also be exogenous influences on the flow of crimes—exogenously driven changes in attitudes on the part of criminals—that for any given level of enforcement effort affect the number of enforcement actions.

There are usually no measures of the flow of background criminal activity nor of the actual (enforced) boundary between acceptable and prohibited behavior; but there are data on enforcement actions, and it is tempting to use the data to infer something about the stringency of enforcement. Those inferences are, however, at best tenuous.

## Goals, Ambiguities, and Dilemmas of Antitrust Policy

The broad goals of antitrust policy should be to encourage greater efficiency in the U.S. economy by checking the inefficiencies that arise from the exercise of market power.[11] But when the exercise of market power may also involve greater production efficiency, trade-offs may be necessary.[12] And where there are alternative explanations for a specific business practice—one increasing efficiency and the other anticompetitive—judgments as to the legitimacy of the practice may be difficult.

Even those who agree with these broad goals for antitrust[13] may differ in their approach to enforcement, because of their differing beliefs or predilections, or both, as to

—the empirical ease of entry, or of expansion by smaller firms, that would constrain the exercise of market power;

—the extent to which oligopolistic coordination can cause sellers in markets where only a few rivals are present to deviate from competitive norms;

—the extent and importance of the efficiency advantages that accompany mergers and larger enterprise size generally;

—the extent and importance of the efficiency advantages that accompany various vertical restraints and other business practices; and

—the importance of longer-run gains in dynamic efficiency versus shorter-run considerations of static efficiency.

11. This is consistent with the positions of Posner (1976); Bork (1978); and Litan and Shapiro (2002).

12. This is illustrated in Williamson (1968). Until the 1970s, regulation was considered the policy solution for instances in which efficiencies were unavoidably accompanied by the exercise of market power. But the difficulties and inefficiencies of regulation led to the deregulation movement of the 1970s and after. See, for example, White (1981b); Joskow and Rose (1989); Noll (1989); Winston (1993); Joskow and Noll (1994).

13. But not all would agree. Some would add a populist element, limiting the absolute size of firms and preserving small ones even at the expense of efficiency; others would favor efficiency when it benefits consumers but not when it benefits producers.

For example, the structural relief policies advocated by Carl Kaysen and Donald Turner were driven by their general skepticism about the prospects for market entry (which in turn were largely driven by the evidence gathered by Joe Bain), their strong concern about oligopolistic coordination, and their skepticism about the significant advantages of size and of vertical restraints and other business practices. The far more restrained policies advocated by Robert Bork reflected his substantially different views in each of these areas.[14] The differing views of the critics and the supporters of the major cases of the Clinton era are usually rooted in such differences in perspectives rather than in differences about underlying goals.

## Uncontroversial (Largely) Antitrust Successes

There were at least five areas of enforcement in which the Clinton antitrust policies scored significant successes that are generally considered uncontroversial.

### Amnesty or Leniency for First Confessors

Active prosecution of horizontal price-fixing conspiracies is an important but often unsung (and underappreciated) task of the Justice Department. These prosecutions were actively pursued by previous administrations, and there generally were no complaints by Democratic critics about this aspect of antitrust enforcement. The Clinton Antitrust Division continued in this tradition and won some high-profile cases (with large criminal fines), including international vitamins, food additives, and related cases and the Sotheby's-Christie's auction commissions conspiracy.

An important enforcement departure, however, was the announcement in August 1993 that the first conspirator to step forward with evidence concerning a price-fixing conspiracy would be eligible for leniency or amnesty in the subsequent prosecution, regardless of whether an investigation had begun. Leniency for the first to confess is general practice when prosecutors have otherwise weak evidence; this practice forms the basis for the well-known prisoner's dilemma of game theory and is familiar from many episodes of television police and prosecution dramas. But previously

14. Bain (1956); Kaysen and Turner (1959); Bork (1978).

the leniency policy had applied only if an investigation had not yet begun. Because the potential confessor often did not know whether an investigation had been opened, the uncertainty discouraged confessions.

The new policy removed that uncertainty. It also freshly promoted the existence and availability of the amnesty or leniency possibility for conspirators with second thoughts. Though it is unclear how important the policy was in helping crack cases, it cannot have hurt and may well have helped. It ought to be a permanent part of the antitrust enforcement policy of all future administrations.

### Merger Guidelines and Merger Enforcement

In 1982 the Justice Department scrapped the *Merger Guidelines* it had issued in 1968 and replaced them with reformulated guidelines, a major contribution of which was a new approach to market definition for merger analysis. The new guidelines were controversial. The state attorneys general, for example, criticized them extensively and proposed their own guidelines. The Justice Department's guidelines were modified modestly in 1984 and again in 1992, when the FTC joined as coauthor and the title was changed to *Horizontal Merger Guidelines*.[15]

The Clinton Justice Department did not scrap or seriously modify these 1992 guidelines. (This contrasted with its early decision to scrap the Reagan Justice Department's *Vertical Restraints Guidelines*, which had been issued in 1985.)[16] The only change to the 1992 guidelines was a small modification in 1997 that attempted to clarify the kinds of evidence of efficiencies that would be considered as an offset to the prospects of market power.

Merger enforcement stringency by the Justice Department and FTC was not appreciably different during the Clinton administration from its predecessors. The guidelines have two (nominal) major decision points with respect to postmerger seller concentration as measured by the Herfindahl-Hirschman Index (HHI). Mergers with postmerger seller concentrations of 1000 or less are unlikely to be challenged. Those with postmerger seller concentrations above 1800, if the merger itself causes an increase in the HHI of 100 or more, are presumed anticompetitive. If the increase in the HHI is between 50 and 100, there is heightened scrutiny of

---

15. For links to the full set of guidelines, see www.doj.gov/atr/hmerger.htm guidelines.
16. U.S. Department of Justice (1985).

a merger. In either event other factors (ease of entry, strong buyer power, difficulties of coordinated seller behavior) can overcome the presumption. For a moderately concentrated market with a postmerger seller concentration between 1000 and 1800 and a merger-based HHI increase of more than 100, the presumption of competitive concern is weaker.

By the late 1980s it was clear that Justice and the FTC were rarely if ever challenging mergers in markets with postmerger HHIs below 2000 and were approving mergers with substantially higher concentrations when the merging parties' claims of offsetting factors carried the day. This pattern continued through the Clinton years. There were, of course, high-profile controversial mergers, some of which were challenged and some approved; but the same had been true before the Clinton administration. As the methodological discussion presented earlier indicated, this pattern of occasional challenges is exactly what would be expected when there are empirical ambiguities and uncertainties about market definition, oligopolistic coordination, conditions of entry, and postmerger efficiencies. The only way to know more precisely whether enforcement stringency changed appreciably during the Clinton years would be to compare the (pre- and post-Clinton) location of the line (in terms of HHI) separating those mergers that were challenged and those that were approved, holding constant the other conditions in the market. Such a study, which would likely require information from the agencies' cutting room floors about investigated but unchallenged mergers, has to my knowledge never been done.

One other aspect of merger enforcement is worth mentioning. Despite an unprecedented wave of mergers during the late 1990s and many headline-grabbing mergers among large companies, the Clinton Justice Department and FTC did not succumb to populist temptations to propose a ban on large conglomerate mergers.[17]

### International Information Exchanges

As companies have become larger and more global, and as many markets have become more global, the extent of U.S. antitrust laws' extraterritorial reach, and even the international extent of investigations and information gathering, became more important. The Clinton Justice Department and FTC successfully urged the passage of the International

17. This contrasts with the Carter Justice Department's endorsement of such a ban during a previous merger wave. See White (1981a, chap.15).

Antitrust Enforcement Cooperation Act of 1994 and cooperated extensively with their counterparts in Canada and the European Union in sharing information during investigations.

However, despite periodic consideration of the possibility, the administration resisted harmonizing U.S. antitrust policy with that of other countries. Although harmonization may ease the conformance burdens on international companies (and has a nice ring to it), it does entail a loss of national sovereignty and the near certainty that the harmonized policy will be different from the policy that the United States would choose unilaterally. Consequently, the administration's resistance was the right choice.

### Competition Advocacy and Amicus Briefs

Though they are generally less well known than their litigation efforts, the Justice Department and the FTC have actively taken positions advocating competition and efficiency in testimony, petitions, and filings before regulatory agencies and have filed amicus briefs in important appellate and Supreme Court cases. The Clinton administration agencies continued the tradition. Following are three examples, all to the good.[18]

THE UNION PACIFIC–SOUTHERN PACIFIC MERGER (1996). In 1995 the Union Pacific railroad proposed merging with the Southern Pacific railroad.[19] Jurisdiction over the merger lay with the Interstate Commerce Commission, to be succeeded by the Surface Transportation Board in 1996. In its consideration of the merger, the ICC-STB accepted filings from interested parties. The Justice Department filed a strong report opposing the merger and pointing out its serious anticompetitive aspects and the shortcomings of its promised efficiencies.[20] Despite the objections of the department and others, the STB approved the merger in July 1996. Within a year, as the UP began to absorb the SP's operations, the merged company experienced serious operational difficulties that at times froze a significant part of the nation's rail network west of the Mississippi and

18. Litan and Shapiro (2002) provide two other examples: the Justice Department's opposition in the 1990s to allowing the Bell operating companies to enter long-distance service until they had shown adequately that they had opened their local service networks to competition, and the department's cooperation with the Securities and Exchange Commission in both agencies' investigation and prosecution of price-fixing in stock quotations on the Nasdaq.

19. Greater detail about this case can be found in Kwoka and White (2004b); White (2002b).

20. Majure (1996).

lasted more than two years, raising serious questions as to the wisdom of the STB's decision.

NRSRO REGULATION. In 1975 the Securities and Exchange Commission created a regulatory category—"nationally recognized statistical rating organization" (NRSRO)—for bond-rating firms whose ratings could be used for the purposes of financial regulation. It immediately grandfathered Moody's, Standard & Poor's, and Fitch into the category.[21] During the next seventeen years it permitted only four more entrants into the category, through informal procedures; but by 2000 the four entrants had merged among themselves and with Fitch, so that only the three original firms remained in the category.[22]

In 1997 the SEC proposed regulations that would formalize its criteria for permitting new firms to enter the NRSRO category (if it ever chose to permit more entrants). The Justice Department filed a letter that pointed out the anticompetitive aspects of the proposed regulations.[23] The SEC has not made the regulations final, and only in February 2003 did it approve one new entrant.

STATE OIL CO. V. KHAN. Resale price maintenance (RPM) is a business practice whereby an "upstream" entity (a manufacturer, for example) specifies the price at which a "downstream" entity (a distributor) can sell its product. Because the manufacturer also sets its own wholesale price on the item, RPM effectively sets the distributor's gross margin on the product. Although retail price maintenance usually consists of a manufacturer's specifying the minimum price that a distributor or retailer can charge, RPM sometimes involves instead the specification of a maximum price. Minimum-price RPM can be a way for the manufacturer to deal with free-riding problems among its distributors—for example, with respect to information-provision and promotion efforts—but it may also serve as a cover for a horizontal price-fixing conspiracy among manufacturers or distributors.[24] Maximum-price RPM is unlikely to be a cover for a conspiracy and can allow a manufacturer to restrain any market power that may be

21. For more detail on this matter see White (2002a).

22. A bond-rating firm that does not have the NRSRO designation is at a severe disadvantage: the participants in the capital markets are much less likely to look to its ratings because the ratings cannot affect financial regulatory outcomes. See White (2002a).

23. U.S. Department of Justice (1998).

24. Telser (1960); White (1981b).

exercised by its distributors (for instance, if they are the sole distributor in a geographic area).

Minimum-price RPM (even by a single manufacturer) has been a per se violation of section 1 of the Sherman Act since 1911[25] and is often loosely described as "vertical price fixing." In 1968 the Supreme Court added maximum-price RPM to the per se violation category.[26] The Court had another opportunity to assess maximum RPM in *State Oil Co.* v. *Khan.*[27] The Justice Department and the Federal Trade Commission filed a joint amicus brief that urged the Court to adopt instead a rule-of-reason approach for maximum RPM. The Court did just that in its decision. Perhaps the day will come when the same can happen to minimum RPM.

### Antitrust Jurisdiction over Pharmaceutical Patent Settlements

Although negotiated settlements of private litigation disputes are often an efficient way of economizing on litigation costs, as well as saving court resources, settlements may sometimes have anticompetitive consequences. For illustration, suppose the holder of an important patent, such as a unique pharmaceutical, that permits its owner to exercise market power is sued by a potential rival, who claims the patent is invalid. (Or the incumbent sues a rival for infringing on the patent.) After some initial discovery the parties reach an agreement: in return for a payment from the incumbent the challenger drops the suit and either goes away or receives a license from the incumbent to sell the patented product on terms that leaves control over the market to the incumbent.

If the challenger's case is weak or is revealed to be so after the initial discovery, the settlement and payment can be an efficient means of hastening the end of pointless and potentially wasteful litigation. But suppose the challenger's case is strong. It is well understood that an incumbent monopolist should be willing to pay more to acquire or defend a crucial asset that preserves its monopoly than a challenger would be willing to pay for the same asset, because the challenger foresees its successful entry as involving a more competitive marketplace. The incumbent would thus find worthwhile the payment of a large sum—up to the amount that the incumbent

---

25. *Dr. Miles Medical Co.* v. *John D. Park & Sons Co.*, 220 U.S. 373 (1911).
26. *Albrech* v. *Herald Co.*, 390 U.S. 145 (1968).
27. *State Oil Co.* v. *Khan,* 522 U.S. 3 (1997). For more detail on this case see Bamberger (2004).

would be expected to lose if the challenger entered—to a challenger with a strong legal case in return for the challenger's agreement to go away, to delay market entry, or to enter on limited terms.[28]

One way to differentiate between the two possibilities is to look at the size of the settlement payment: if it is close to the size of the litigation expenses saved, efficient settlement seems likely; if it is appreciably higher than the litigation costs saved and approaches a significant fraction of the incumbent's rents from a continued unchallenged position, the collusive settlement scenario becomes more likely. In the late 1990s the FTC challenged a number of patent settlement cases that it believed fit the latter interpretation of the settlements. These challenges are likely to—and should—continue.

## The Controversial Cases

The Clinton Justice Department and FTC pursued some cases that arguably would not have been initiated by their predecessors. This section discusses nine of the most important. A frequent theme is raising rivals' costs.[29]

### Microsoft

The *Microsoft* case was the highest-profile case of the Clinton era. It was really two somewhat related actions, the second of which made front-page headlines.

THE FIRST CASE. In 1990 the FTC opened an investigation of the proposed plan by Microsoft and IBM to develop jointly future operating systems.[30] When the plans later unraveled, the FTC's staff turned its attention to Microsoft's marketing practices, about which there had been many complaints by software rivals.

Three issues were prominent. First, Microsoft's contracts with some personal computer makers (often termed original equipment manufacturers, or OEMs) required them to pay a fee for every personal computer that

---

28. The intricacies of federal pharmaceutical patent legislation add some extra protections for the incumbent in such instances. For a discussion see Gilbert and Tom (2001); Litan and Shapiro (2002).

29. Salop and Scheffman (1983, 1987).

30. For further discussion see White (1994); Gilbert (1999).

was shipped, regardless of whether Microsoft's operating systems were installed on all of them. Some contracts ran for as long as five years. These practices raised barriers to entry (raised rivals' costs) by making it harder for a rival operating systems company to convince a manufacturer to experiment with or sample its system. Second, Microsoft was allowing some applications software developers to have early access to its Windows operating system but requiring that the developers not collaborate with other producers of operating systems for up to three years. Again, this raised rivals' costs and barriers to entry. Third, software applications rivals complained that Microsoft's vertical integration of operating systems production and software application production gave it an unfair advantage in the development of the software applications.[31]

In February 1993 the FTC deadlocked in a 2-2 vote as to whether to issue an order that would restrain Microsoft's behavior. Another vote in July again yielded a 2-2 tie. The Department of Justice, however, in a virtually unprecedented action, decided to continue the investigation. In July 1994 the department and Microsoft reached an agreement on a consent decree concerning the first two practices.[32] The company agreed that its contracts with OEMs would require that they pay only for Microsoft operating systems shipped on their PCs and that the contracts would run for no longer than a year. Microsoft also agreed that its testing arrangements with applications software developers would not prevent the developers from working with other operating systems producers as long as confidential information was not revealed and that these agreements would not last longer than a year. The third issue, concerning Microsoft's vertical integration into applications software, was left unaddressed.

Critics of the consent decree (many of them software applications developers) complained that the decree did little to address Microsoft's basic market power in either operating systems or applications software. They convinced Judge Stanley Sporkin to stay the decree in February 1995, but the decision was overturned four months later by the District of Columbia Circuit Court of Appeals, and the decree came into effect.[33]

An incidental provision of the decree, which was not central to its major thrust, restricted Microsoft from tying other software products to its

---

31. Microsoft argued that there were efficiency justifications for all these practices.

32. Simultaneously Microsoft reached a similar agreement with the European Union's Competition Directorate.

33. *United States* v. *Microsoft Corp.*, 159 F.R.D. 318 (1995); *United States* v. *Microsoft Corp.*, 56 F.3d 1448 (1995).

operating system. But the decree did not prevent Microsoft from selling integrated products. The tension between these two provisions led to the second and more substantial Microsoft case.

THE SECOND CASE. In October 1997 the Justice Department sued Microsoft, claiming that the company was violating the terms of the consent decree by tying its browser, the Internet Explorer, to its Windows operating system.[34] After an initial victory in federal district court the department lost after Microsoft appealed to the District of Columbia Circuit Court of Appeals.[35] In the meantime it had reformulated its case into a more general Sherman Act section 2 tying and monopolization case, which it filed in May 1998. The department was joined in this suit by nineteen state attorneys general. The case, handled by Judge Thomas Penfield Jackson, went to trial in spring 1999. Judge Jackson issued his findings of fact in November, largely siding with the department and the states.[36] He then asked Judge Richard A. Posner to mediate, but Judge Posner was unable to find sufficient common ground among the parties. Judge Jackson issued his "Conclusions of Law" in April 2000, which found Microsoft guilty.[37] Two months later he ordered the company to be broken into two separate companies: an operating systems company and an applications software plus browser company.

Microsoft again appealed to the D.C. Circuit Court of Appeals, and in June 2001 the court, with seven judges sitting en banc, decided unanimously that Microsoft was guilty of violating section 2 of the Sherman Act for the reasons discussed later, though it overturned Judge Jackson's dissolution order.[38] In the fall of 2001 the Justice Department and about half of the states signed a consent decree with Microsoft; but nine states wanted a tougher remedy, and their pursuit of that remedy delayed a final settlement. In November 2002 Judge Colleen Kollar-Kotelly approved the settlement, but two states have chosen to appeal that decision.[39]

34. For further details and arguments see Evans and others (2000); Brennan (2001); Gilbert and Katz (2001); Klein (2001); Whinston (2001); White (2001); Rubinfeld (2004).

35. *United States* v. *Microsoft Corp.*, 980 F. Supp. 537 (1997); *U.S.* v. *Microsoft Corp.*, 147 F.3d 935 (1998).

36. *United States* v. *Microsoft Corp.*, 84 F. Supp.2d 9 (1999).

37. *United States* v. *Microsoft Corp.*, 87 F. Supp.2d 30 (2000).

38. *United States* v. *Microsoft Corp.*, 253 F.3d 34 (2001). The unanimous decision included Judge Douglas Ginsburg, who had been the Assistant Attorney General for Antitrust during the middle of the Reagan administration.

39. *United States* v. *Microsoft Corp.*, 231 F.Supp.2d (2002).

Although the Justice Department has at times not presented its story as coherently as one might like, the essential features of its case are as follows (this summary is consistent with the circuit court's opinion).[40]

—With an 80–90 percent share of the operating systems market, Microsoft has had and continues to have market power. The claim that software markets were dynamic and fluid, with market power fleeting at best, was not valid for this case.[41]

—A buttressing of that market power comes from the installed base or applications barrier to entry. Because PC users care about having large numbers of applications software programs available and compatible with their operating systems, because the switching costs to a new (incompatible) system are substantial, and because software applications developers would write their software primarily for the dominant system (and creating compatibility with, or "porting to," other systems was costly), any smaller systems producer or potential entrant was placed at a severe disadvantage. Far fewer software applications would be available for use alongside any entrant operating system.

—In 1995 and 1996 Microsoft saw the combination of the Netscape Navigator browser plus Sun Microsystems' Java flexible programming language ("write once, run anywhere") as a strong threat to its market power in the operating systems market. If applications software developers saw the Navigator-Java combination as the major platform for using the World Wide Web, they would begin writing software so that it would be compatible with the Navigator-Java combination. Other operating systems producers would only have to make their systems compatible with the Navigator-Java combination and would be at a lesser installed-base disadvantage.

—Microsoft offered a market-sharing arrangement to Netscape in June 1995, but Netscape refused.

—Microsoft then went out of its way to make life difficult for Netscape: by tying the Internet Explorer, its newly developed browser, to its operating system and then technologically integrating it into Windows; by insisting that manufacturers not delete it and not feature or distribute the Netscape Navigator; by inducing Intel to cease work on software that could make entry by other operating systems producers easier; and by forcing

40. On coherence see, for example, the critique in Brennan (2001).
41. The Department of Justice similarly rejected such arguments in objecting to Microsoft's proposal to acquire Intuit in 1995. For a discussion of that case see Horvitz (1996).

Internet service providers to feature Internet Explorer and not Netscape Navigator. These actions raised a rival's costs with a vengeance.

—Microsoft also made Java a less-than-universal language by developing its own version of Java that was incompatible with other operating systems, thereby weakening the universality and overall attractiveness of the Navigator-Java combination.[42]

In essence, then, a dominant firm in an operating systems market where entry was difficult was going out of its way to disadvantage a firm that produced a complementary product because that product could provide the basis for a major challenge to the dominant firm's core market power position. It was thereby raising its rival's costs, buttressing its core position, and likely deterring future such entrants. Seen this way Microsoft's actions, on the heels of the behavior that had been the basis for the consent decree in the first case, constituted a serious violation of section 2 of the Sherman Act and deserved the challenge it received.

### American Airlines

Perhaps the second most controversial case initiated during the Clinton administration was the Justice Department's predatory behavior case against American Airlines.[43]

In the two and a half decades since the Airline Deregulation Act of 1978, few new airlines have been able to sustain themselves as serious rivals to the large incumbent airlines. Partly the hub-and-spokes route structure that developed shortly after deregulation has proved to be an effective way of taking advantage of the network economies of an air transport system. Entrants find these economies difficult to replicate, but they have also found that incumbent carriers have dropped their prices and expanded their flight frequencies in city-pair markets in response to new competition, only to reverse course after the entrant ceases serving the city pair. The entrants and their champions have frequently cried "predation." In response the Department of Transportation proposed regulations that would have set limits on such behavior, but it backed away from final promulgation.

---

42. Microsoft defended its actions by arguing that it did not have market power, that there were efficiency and customer convenience justifications for what it did, and that there was no consumer harm. See, for example, Evans and others (2000); Klein (2001).

43. Edlin and Farrell (2004) provide further discussion.

Predation has been a troubling issue for antitrust. In principle the concept is clear: in a market in which, for example, a dominant firm exercises market power and in which entry is difficult, the dominant firm may find it worthwhile to set prices or product offerings or both in a way that is designed specifically to drive a smaller rival from the market. It does so in the expectation that after the rival's exit the dominant firm becomes even more dominant and its prices can be raised to recoup whatever sacrifices were entailed in chasing the rival away. The incumbent also achieves a reputation for chasing away entrants, which will discourage future entry in this or other markets and thus adds to the financial recovery from the initial actions. This investment-cum-recovery scenario is often presented in terms of pricing, but it can apply to nonprice behavior as well.[44] However, it may be difficult to distinguish between such predatory behavior and simply aggressive competitive behavior, which the antitrust laws ought not to discourage.

In an effort to forestall such discouragements of aggressive but legitimate competitive behavior, Philip Areeda and Donald Turner suggested a rule that prices at or above variable costs per unit should be considered a "safe harbor" defense against predation claims.[45] Their rule was at least partly in response to legal and regulatory decisions that claimed that predation occurred when prices were below average costs (or below "fully allocated costs," with the joint costs of a multiproduct company being allocated in some wholly arbitrary fashion). But the Areeda-Turner rule would nevertheless protect some truly predatory pricing forays. And it has no natural nonprice analog.

As a more general rule Janusz Ordover and Robert Willig have devised an approach that asks, was the dominant firm's action the more profitable choice for it *only* on the assumption that the rival would exit (and costs could be recouped)?[46] Equivalently, on the assumption instead that the rival would remain in the market, was there another course of action known at the time (other than the one that the dominant firm actually took) that would have been more profitable? If the answer to this question is yes, the action was predatory.

---

44. *Microsoft* can also be interpreted through this lens—that the company's actions constituted an investment in anticipation of recouping costs that would occur because of a strengthened position in the operating systems market because of a weakened Netscape.

45. Areeda and Turner (1975).

46. Ordover and Willig (1981, 1999).

Against this backdrop let us review the American Airlines case. In 1995–97 American faced competition from small low-cost entrants (Vanguard, Western Pacific, and SunJet) on a few of the routes to and from its major hub, Dallas–Fort Worth International Airport. In response to their entry American lowered its prices to meet the entrants' prices. American also expanded its flight frequencies, and it entered a route, DFW–Long Beach, California, that it had previously abandoned as unprofitable but that was being served by SunJet. In each instance the entrant failed to survive, and after its exit "American generally resumed its prior marketing strategy, and in certain markets reduced the number of flights and raised its prices, roughly to levels comparable to those prior to the period of low-fare competition."[47]

The Justice Department sued American in May 1999 under section 2 of the Sherman Act, claiming that its actions were predatory. The department did *not* claim that American's pricing actions alone were predatory. Instead, it claimed as predatory American's second-stage expansions of low-fare seat availability and capacity—that the expansions made no business sense unless they would cause the other airlines to exit from their city-pair markets and that American knew that simply lowering fares to meet those of the entrants would be more profitable if the entrants did not exit.

In response American claimed that its prices were at or above route-level variable unit costs, the routes remained profitable, it had matched but not undercut the entrants' prices, and the department's theory of recoupment was speculative. In early 2001 American filed for summary judgment, and in April 2001 Judge J. Thomas Marten granted it.[48] The department has appealed this decision to the Tenth Circuit Court of Appeals. An appellate decision has not yet been issued.

It is important that predatory behavior cases not deteriorate into cases that simply protect inefficient entrants and discourage aggressive competitive behavior. Accordingly, such cases should be reserved for situations in which there is a dominant firm or seller concentration is very high, where entry is difficult, and where recovering costs in the same market in the future or in related markets is a realistic possibility.[49] Further, the Ordover-Willig test is a superior tool for identifying predatory behavior, especially

47. *United States.* v. *AMR Corp. et al.*, 140 F.Supp. 2d 1141, 1144 (2001).

48. *United States* v. *AMR Corp.*, 1141.

49. There is an interesting and important empirical question as to how the effects of building a reputation for not tolerating entrants can be measured and quantified.

of the nonprice sort. In these respects *American Airlines* qualifies as an important case that pushes these ideas into the judicial arena. It definitely should have been initiated.

### Visa and MasterCard

The Visa and MasterCard credit card networks are worldwide associations of thousands of banks. Many, especially in the United States, belong to both networks and issue the cards of both. The Justice Department's suit, brought in 1998, alleged two important (but largely unrelated) points. First, the networks allowed banks that were major issuers of credit cards in one network to be on the board of directors of the other network. This governance structure, the department argued, dulled competition between the two networks and especially dulled innovation. Second, since the early 1990s both networks had had rules that prohibited their U.S. members from issuing the cards of any other network, except that Visa permitted its member banks to issue MasterCards and vice versa. This limited exclusivity (or "duality") made entry or expansion by other card networks more difficult (raising rivals' costs) because banks were important issuers.

The case was tried in federal district court in 2000, and in April 2001 Judge Barbara S. Jones found for the card networks on the governance issue but found for the Justice Department on the matter of restricted exclusivity.[50] The department has decided that it will not appeal its loss on the matter of governance, but Visa and MasterCard are appealing their loss on the exclusivity ruling. Both issues were worth raising and pursuing.

### Intel

In June 1998 the Federal Trade Commission initiated an administrative proceeding against Intel, contending that the company had abused its position of market power in microprocessors by withdrawing from arrangements to share information with three of its customers: Intergraph Corporation, Digital Equipment Corporation, and Compaq. The FTC claimed that Intel's behavior discouraged the three companies from developing technology that might offer competition to Intel in microprocessors. Intel responded that the companies were engaged in legal challenges

50. *United States v. Visa U.S.A. Inc., et al.*, 163 F.Supp.2d 322 (2001).

to its intellectual property rights on its microprocessors and that it could legitimately protect this property, including refusing to deal with them.

The FTC's charges were settled with a consent order in which Intel agreed that it would continue to provide its trade secrets and advance product samples to customers that were suing it for patent infringement, but its obligation ceased if the customer sought an injunction against Intel's manufacture and sale of its microprocessors (which is what Intel cared most about).

Because the Intel action was brought at about the same time the Justice Department was litigating its Microsoft case, questions were raised as to whether the enforcement agencies were hostile to the leading firms in high-technology industries and "the New Economy." But like many of the other cases discussed in this section, a focus on raising rivals' costs puts the case in a less hostile framework.[51]

### Toys "R" Us

During the early 1990s Toys "R" Us, the largest retailer of toys in the United States, persuaded leading toy manufacturers to restrict the range of toys that they sold to a category of its competitors: so-called warehouse clubs—low-cost, high volume retailers. TRU's goal was to restrict the competition that it faced from these retailers in selling popular toys. In May 1996 the Federal Trade Commission charged that the company's efforts constituted an illegal vertical restraint and also that TRU had become the communications hub in a "hub-and-spokes" horizontal conspiracy among the toy manufacturers (each of whom needed assurance that the others were going along) to restrict sales to the warehouse clubs.[52]

TRU's defense was that it did not have market power in retailing toys (or in the purchase of toys from manufacturers), that it provided valuable promotion services for the toys, that the warehouse clubs were free riders on those services, and thus TRU was justified in obtaining restrictions on sales of competitive toys to them.

The case was initially heard by an FTC administrative law judge, who ruled in favor of the agency's charges in September 1997.[53] TRU appealed

---

51. For further discussion of this case see Litan and Shapiro (2002); Pitofsky (2002a); Shapiro (2004).

52. For further discussion of this case see Carlton and Sider (1999); Scherer (2004).

53. *In the Matter of Toys "R" Us*, initial decision, September 25, 1997.

to the full commission, which decided unanimously in 1998 that the company had indeed violated the antitrust laws.[54] TRU then appealed to the Seventh Circuit Court, which in August 2000 affirmed the FTC's decision, finding that the company's vertical efforts and its role in the horizontal boycott had violated section 5 of the Federal Trade Commission Act and section 1 of the Sherman Act.[55]

TRU's actions can be interpreted loosely as an effort to achieve a resale price maintenance arrangement. A frequent efficiency justification for RPM is that it is a way of dealing with the problem of free-riding by rivals on information services provided at the point of sale.[56] This was indeed a major part of TRU's defense, but three layers of judicial review were unconvinced, pointing out that the toy manufacturers paid for advertising, warehousing, and other services.[57] Further, the horizontal conspiracy aspect of the case (TRU assured each of the toy manufacturers that it was talking to the others and telling them the same things) is troubling.[58] And these multilateral assurances undermine the free-riding argument: if each manufacturer valued the services that TRU provided for promoting its toys, the manufacturer should not have needed assurance that the others were participating.

Also, as an alternative to the free-riding argument, the possibility that RPMs might be used to cover a conspiracy among the initiators has been generally acknowledged.[59] Here, though, the initiator was a single firm (and it orchestrated a conspiracy among its suppliers). But if that firm has sufficient market power to get its suppliers to cooperate in disadvantaging its rivals, then a single initiator can well replace a conspiracy of initiators.[60]

However, as is true in many vertical restraints cases, there remains a fuzzy border between illegal activity and the promise in *United States* v. *Colgate* that "in the absence of any purpose to create or maintain a monopoly, [the Sherman Act ] does not restrict the long recognized right of trader or manufacturer engaged in an entirely private business, freely to exercise

---

54. *In the matter of Toys "R" Us*, Opinion of the Commission, 126 FTC 415 (1998).

55. *Toys "R" Us, Inc.* v. *Federal Trade Commission*, 221 F.3d 928 (2000).

56. Telser (1960).

57. There might still be elements of TRU's reputation for stocking worthwhile toys that could be costly to the company and could be important to toy manufacturers, but for which they do not directly reimburse TRU.

58. The case carries the echoes of *Interstate Circuit, Inc., et al.* v. *United States*, 305 U.S. 223 (1939).

59. Telser (1960).

60. As was true in *Interstate Circuit, Inc., et al.* v. *United States*, 306 U.S. 223 (1939); *Klor's, Inc.* v. *Broadway-Hale Stores, Inc.*, 359 U.S. 207 (1959).

his own independent discretion as to parties with whom he will deal. And, of course, he may announce in advance the circumstances under which he will refuse to sell."[61] Suppose that TRU had simply told each manufacturer that it would not buy toys that were also sold to the warehouse clubs? Or what if TRU simply did not buy such toys but let the manufacturers figure out why? Or suppose TRU bought a few such toys but stocked them in the back of their stores where the lighting was dim? What then? The boundaries between acceptable and illegal vertical behavior will surely continue to bedevil antitrust law.

### Dentsply

In January 1999 the Department of Justice filed suit against Dentsply International, charging that this manufacturer of artificial teeth had refused to sell them to dealers who carried certain competing lines and that these actions impaired the ability of the other manufacturers to develop or maintain an adequate dealer network and raised barriers to entry.[62] In April 2000 Dentsply moved for summary judgment, arguing that rival manufacturers could use other channels of distribution and that its dealers could cease carrying its teeth at any time and carry those of other manufacturers instead. In March 2001 Judge Susan L. Robinson denied Dentsply's motion.[63] The case went to trial in April 2002; a decision is awaited. This was another important case involving the raising of rivals' costs.

### Staples and Office Depot

In September 1996 Staples, which had the largest U.S. chain of office supply superstores, proposed to buy Office Depot, the next largest chain.[64] At first, the merger appeared competitively benign, since the two chains together accounted for less than 10 percent of all office supplies sold nationally. But FTC compilations of simple price comparisons among metropolitan areas of some standard office supply products showed that prices charged by Staples or Office Depot were highest where either was the sole superstore chain in the area, lower where there were two chains, and lower

---

61. *United States* v. *Colgate & Co.*, 250 U.S. 300, 307 (1919).

62. For further discussion of this case see Litan and Shapiro (2002); Katz (2002).

63. 2001-1 Trade Cas. (CCH), para.73247.

64. For further discussion of this case see Baker (1999); Dalkir and Warren-Boulton (2004); White (2002).

still where three chains were present.[65] More sophisticated econometrics supported these simple price comparisons.[66]

These results showed that office supply chains were a separate product market and that metropolitan areas were a relevant geographic market; and they showed that the merger would likely have anticompetitive consequences for those metropolitan areas where Staples and Office Depot were both present (and where the merger would thus have a three-firms-to-two or a two-to-one structural outcome). Further, the commission was highly skeptical toward the efficiency claims offered by the merger partners. Following the commission's rejection of a divestiture offer by the companies, it voted to seek a preliminary injunction in April 1997. The case went to trial in June 1997, and at the end of the month Judge Thomas Hogan ruled in favor of the FTC.[67]

The Staples case was important for demonstrating the way in which simple but powerful price comparison data could empirically define markets and show the potential for anticompetitive outcomes.

### MCI WorldCom and Sprint

In October 1999 MCI WorldCom and Sprint, the second and third largest long-distance telephone companies in the United States, announced their intention to merge.[68] The companies were also the first and second largest providers of Internet backbone service. The Department of Justice opposed the merger, arguing that only AT&T, MCI WorldCom, and Sprint had the nationwide telephone networks that were important for customers and that these big three were a separate market from the smaller long-distance carriers that had emerged in the 1980s and 1990s. In essence the department contended that for telephone service, separately for the mass market of residential and small business customers and for the large business market, this was a three-to-two merger and was anticompetitive. The department was also concerned about Internet backbone service, arguing that the combined company would become dominant and could refuse to interconnect with other providers, thereby strengthening its dominance yet further. The European Commission was similarly concerned.

---

65. In addition to Staples and Office Depot, there was one other significant office supply chain: OfficeMax.

66. For some disputation concerning these results see Hausman and Leonard (n.d.); Baker (1999).

67. *Federal Trade Commission* v. *Staples, Inc.*, 970 F.Supp. 1066 (1997).

68. For further discussion of this case see Pelcovits (2004).

MCI WorldCom and Sprint replied in their defense that the smaller companies in the telephone business would discipline any efforts to raise prices above competitive levels, that the merger would achieve significant economies for the merged entity, and that they were willing to divest Sprint's share of the Internet backbone service.

The Justice Department was not convinced by the parties' arguments and in June 2000 announced that it would oppose the merger. About the same time the European Commission announced that it did not believe the spun-off Internet backbone capacity would result in competition as strong as it would be under the ownership of a freestanding Sprint; the EC too opposed the merger.[69]

In the face of this opposition the proposed partners called off the merger rather than contest the matter in court. In the wake of the subsequent accounting debacle and bankruptcy filing by MCI WorldCom in 2002, it was widely believed that the failure of this merger to go forward was crucial to that outcome. The merger momentum of the company was slowed, which revealed its underlying weak management, poor cost controls, and poor profitability. The accounting manipulations by senior executives were a desperate effort to cover these inadequacies.

### Heinz and Beech-Nut

Virtually all jarred baby food is produced by three companies: Gerber, Heinz, and Beech-Nut. Gerber dominates with about two-thirds of the market; the other two split the remainder, with Heinz, though it is perceived by consumers as a value brand, having a slightly greater market share than Beech-Nut, which is perceived as a premium brand.

In February 2000 Heinz proposed to acquire Beech-Nut.[70] The parties argued that their competition with each other was very limited and that their ability to compete with Gerber was restricted as well: Heinz by its value-brand image, Beech-Nut by its antiquated production facilities and high costs, and both by their respective (largely nonoverlapping) regional

---

69. This resembled the position that the department had adopted in Microsoft's proposal to acquire Intuit in 1995. When Microsoft proposed to spin off its Money software (which competed with Intuit's Quicken) as a possible way to make the acquisition palatable, the department responded that the spin-off would mean that Money would be in weaker hands and thus constitute less competitive threat to Quicken than was true under the status quo. In the face of the department's opposition, the proposed acquisition was withdrawn.

70. For further discussion of this case see Baker (2004).

orientations and lack of nationwide presence. They contended that this merger would provide Beech-Nut with access to Heinz's low-cost production technology and allow Heinz to go forward with two innovative ideas in producing baby food that were more likely to be successful if marketed nationwide under the Beech-Nut name (which would occur after the merger because Heinz would convert all its production and sales to the Beech-Nut brand name).

Thus the parties argued that even though the proposal appeared to be a three-to-two merger with a very high HHI resulting, competition would actually be invigorated because the combined company would be able to compete aggressively against Gerber in ways that neither could before. The lower production costs and important innovations gave them an incentive to expand sales by reducing prices rather than tacitly colluding with Gerber at higher prices but reduced volume.

The FTC was not convinced. It argued that there was significant wholesale competition between the parties for space on supermarkets' shelves and saw postmerger concentration as very high (the nationwide HHI would rise by 510 points to 5285) with enormous entry barriers. And the commission was suspicious of the parties' efficiency claims, contending that those efficiencies might well be achievable by the parties without a merger. In July 2000 it voted to seek a preliminary injunction to stop the merger. The manufacturers contested the action, and in October after a five-day trial in late August and early September, Judge James Robertson sided with the merging parties, largely accepting their arguments.[71] The commission appealed to the D.C. Circuit Court of Appeals. In April 2001 a unanimous panel reversed the district court and supported the agency.[72]

The Heinz case illustrates the dilemma faced by judicial analysis of merger plans when postmerger market concentration is high: how and when to accept the merging parties' promises of resulting efficiencies. Before a merger, promises are easy to make, but certainty of postmerger follow-through is impossible. In addition, unexpected problems in combining two disparate organizations (as clearly was the case in the Union Pacific–Southern Pacific merger) may foil even the best-intended plans for achieving new efficiencies.

---

71. *Federal Trade Commission* v. *H . J. Heinz Co.*, 116 F.Supp.2d 190 (2000).
72. *Federal Trade Commission* v. *H. J. Heinz Co.*, 246 F.3d 708 (2001).

## Disappointments and Missed Opportunities

The Clinton administration's antitrust efforts were also marked by a number of notable disappointments and missed opportunities. The following are the most important of these instances.

### Bell Atlantic and NYNEX

In April 1996 Bell Atlantic and NYNEX, the two large and contiguous providers of local telephone service along the eastern seaboard—NYNEX, from Maine through New York and Bell Atlantic from New Jersey through Virginia—announced an agreement to merge.[73] The merger was reviewed by the Department of Justice, Federal Communications Commission, and thirteen state regulatory commissions. In April 1997 Justice announced that it would not object to the merger. The thirteen state commissions also cleared it. In August 1997, after examining the merger against a public interest standard, the FCC insisted on some commitments by the two parties that would (arguably) make entry into local service easier for smaller companies and then approved the merger.

A crucial antitrust issue was whether Bell Atlantic was an important potential entrant into NYNEX's local service markets, especially New York City and its suburbs. There was a strong case that Bell Atlantic was the best situated entrant and the most likely to be successful.[74] Further, by early 1997 it was clear that one of the major promises of the proponents of the Telecommunications Act of 1996—that the act would open up competition in local service markets—was greatly overstated. A challenge to the merger on the grounds that competition would potentially be reduced would have been worthwhile. It might well have succeeded, and Bell Atlantic might today be competing with its own facilities against NYNEX in New York and other Northeast cities.

### Hospital Mergers

Both the Justice Department and the Federal Trade Commission have lost a string of actions against hospital mergers. Competition in local markets

---

73. For more details on this matter see Brenner (2004).
74. Brenner (2004).

among hospitals does matter, even in the presence of health insurance for patients, because hospitals can compete for health insurance contracts and for affiliations with local physicians. It is a disappointment that the agencies have not been more convincing in their judicial arguments.

### California Dental Association

In July 1993 the Federal Trade Commission filed an administrative complaint against the California Dental Association, charging that it had violated section 5 of the FTC Act by placing unreasonable restrictions on its members' advertising of price and quality claims.[75] An FTC administrative law judge supported the charge in July 1995. The association appealed to the full commission, which in March 1996 determined that the association's actions did indeed violate the FTC Act.[76]

California Dental then appealed to the Ninth Circuit Court of Appeals, which by a 2-1 vote supported the FTC's decision in July 1997.[77] An issue in the appeal was whether the agency was required to conduct a full-scale rule-of-reason analysis or whether a briefer ("quick-look," "truncated," "abbreviated," or "structured rule-of-reason") inquiry was sufficient for this type of allegation. The court affirmed that the commission's abbreviated inquiry had been sufficient.

California Dental appealed to the Supreme Court, which granted certiorari and in May 1999 on a 5-4 vote reversed the appellate court and remanded the case to the Ninth Circuit.[78] The Supreme Court majority argued that the FTC's inquiry had not been sufficient. On remand the Ninth Circuit Court of Appeals gave more credence to CDA's arguments and directed that the commission drop the case.[79] In early 2001 the FTC decided not to appeal, and the court dismissed the case.

Because the Supreme Court had endorsed the quick-look approach in other cases, its reversal here was somewhat surprising and certainly dis-

---

75. For further discussion of this case see Calkins (2000); Muris (2000).

76. *In re California Dental Association*, 121 F.T.C. 190 (1996).

77. *California Dental Association* v. *Federal Trade Commission*, 128 F.3d 720 (1997).

78. *California Dental Association* v. *Federal Trade Commission*, 526 U.S. 756 (1999). The other issue on appeal was whether the FTC had jurisdiction over the association because it is nonprofit. The circuit court had said that the commission did have jurisdiction, and the Supreme Court unanimously affirmed that position.

79. *California Dental Association* v. *Federal Trade Commission*, 224 F.3d 942 (2000).

tressing.[80] A full-scale rule-of-reason trial is costly and should be avoided when the plaintiff can combine theory and evidence to support a strong presumption that the practice is anticompetitive. Unfortunately, the FTC chose not to provide much in the way of evidence. It did not ask an economist to testify, there was no empirical evidence on the adverse effects of the restraints, no evidence to define local markets, and no evidence on the defendant's market power. These were all strategic case management decisions by the commission.[81] That it failed to provide sufficient evidence to convince the Supreme Court may prove to have been a costly error indeed.

### Aluminum Producers

In 1993 the American and European aluminum producers were complaining about overcapacity in the industry and the prevailing low prices, both of which were largely attributable to Russian aluminum producers' entering world markets. Political pressure to do something intensified. The trade representatives of the United States, the European Union, Norway, Canada, Australia, and Russia met in late 1993 and early 1994 to try to compromise on a cartel-like agreement that would reduce capacity. They finally agreed in late January 1994.[82]

Trade restrictions and good antitrust policy are almost always antithetical. As usual, there were political arguments in defense of the cartel agreement: that it forestalled antidumping filings by U.S. aluminum companies, and some equivalent actions in Europe, that would have been worse. Perhaps. But antidumping actions are (unfortunately) by now a regular part of the political landscape. Cartel agreements are not, and ought not to become so. This was a big step, with a big risk, in the wrong direction.

Although the Clinton antitrust enforcement agencies may not have been directly involved, the aluminum cartel was nevertheless a step backward for antitrust principles.

---

80. See for comparison *National Society of Professional Engineers* v. *United States*, 435 U.S. 679 (1978); *NCAA* v. *Board of Regents of the University of Oklahoma*, 468 U.S. 85 (1984); *Federal Trade Commission* v. *Indiana Federation of Dentists*, 476 U.S. 447 (1986).

81. By contrast, in *Massachusetts Board of Registration in Optometry*, 110 FTC 549 (1988), which was also a "quick look" case, the commission offered much more evidence.

82. Martin Du Bois and Eric Norton, "Aluminum Pact Is Set to Curb World Output," *Wall Street Journal*, January 31, 1994, p. A3.

*Vertical Restraints*

Recall that a Department of Justice action early during the Clinton administration was to rescind the *Vertical Restraints Guidelines* that had been issued in 1985. Unfortunately, neither Justice nor the FTC during the 1990s issued anything to replace them.

Vertical restraints have been and continue to be a difficult problem for antitrust policy. Partly this is a terminological problem: many of the words and phrases in vertical restraint discussions—"tying," "foreclosure," "exclusive dealing," "refusal to deal"—have a somewhat sinister sound and are easily (if often mistakenly) transformed by plaintiffs' counsel into anticompetitive pejoratives. Partly the problem is analytical confusion: vertical practices are sometimes confusing, and it may be difficult to ascertain exactly who is doing what to whom. And partly there are usually two or more possible explanations for or interpretations of a vertical practice: it may promote efficiency by dealing with free riding, restricting opportunistic behavior, or reducing transactions costs; but it may also raise rivals' costs. If the cost increases have a significant effect on the market, the practice deserves closer scrutiny.

It would have been (and still would be) valuable to have publicly available analytically rigorous principles that the Justice Department and the FTC could use in deciding when to bring cases that involve vertical matters (whether restraints or mergers). Pointing out the analytical similarities among many of the vertical practices that have different names should be part of this effort.[83] The presence and extent of market power as a starting point for any serious legal consideration ought to be another component.[84] Smart lawyers and economists at the enforcement agencies could surely find more principles that could provide valuable guidance for the private sector and contribute to the orderly development of judicial decisions. It is a disappointment that the Clinton agencies did not try to do so.

*Market Definition in Monopolization Cases*

Since the early 1980s antitrust economics has operated without guidelines to the definition of the market in monopolization cases, including

83. White (1989).

84. But see the discussion in the next section. Also, an insistence on the presence of market power would call into question the per se treatment of minimum RPM, or at least put it into the same category as the per se treatment of tying. But that would be all to the good.

cases involving vertical restraints and predatory behavior.[85] As a precursor to a monopolization case, one must find that the defendant is exercising market power; and to do that, one must generally specify a market.

The 1982 *Merger Guidelines* (and subsequent revisions) laid out a paradigm that has proved durable for analyzing prospective mergers. It asks whether a group of sellers, if they acted jointly as a monopolist, could successfully increase prices from their current (or otherwise likely future) levels by at least a small but significant amount. In essence the paradigm defines a market as a group of sellers that has the potential to act as a monopoly.

But that paradigm generally cannot be used to define a market when the charge is that the defendant already exercises market power (and the charged act has created or increased exercise of that power).[86] The reason lies in the heart of microeconomics monopoly theory: if a monopolist is maximizing profits, it is maintaining its price at a level consistent with that maximization. To ask whether the price could be raised even higher to increase profits is to ask a question to which the answer—even for a monopolist—ought always to be no. Equivalently, a price increase test for asking whether a company is exercising market power commits the "cellophane fallacy."[87] A monopolist and a competitive company should both be expected to answer the question no, and thus the question cannot distinguish between the two.

Until the early 1980s a primary source of evidence supporting claims of monopolization and thus of addressing the problem of market definition question was profitability data. Thus, for example, in contrast with du Pont's claim that it did not exercise market power in cellophane in the 1940s because it had only a small share—about 17 percent—of the flexible wrapping materials market, George Stocking and Willard Mueller argued that du Pont indeed had market power in cellophane (and thus cellophane was a relevant market) by comparing its reported profits producing and selling cellophane with the much lower profits it reported producing and selling rayon (where it had a comparable market share and faced fifteen to eighteen rival firms).[88] Through the 1970s a major component of monopolization cases was profit rates.

85. This section draws on White (1999, 2000).

86. As Werden (2000) points out, however, the *Merger Guidelines* paradigm could be used to define a market where the charge is that the defendant's prospective actions will allow it to monopolize the market.

87. Derived from the Supreme Court's mistaken asking of this question in *United States* v. *E. I. du Pont de Nemours and Co.*, 351 U.S. 377 (1956); see Stocking and Mueller (1955).

88. On the market share in rayon see Markham (1952). Stocking and Mueller (1955) also examine du Pont's business strategy for cellophane and its pricing patterns.

This line of analysis received a serious blow from studies by George Benston and by Franklin Fisher and John McGowan, who argued that standard accounting data could not be trusted to reveal the excess profits that would be expected from the exercise of market power.[89] Shaken by these arguments, economists reduced their use of profit data as indicators of the exercise of market power. But they developed no general paradigm to replace these data.

Sometimes sufficient price data may be available and can be used to delineate markets and indicate the presence or absence of the exercise of market power.[90] Or there may be unique features of the product and its environment that can help delineate the market. Still, the excess profits (rents) component of the economists' standard monopoly paradigm has been severely hobbled as an empirical tool. But because nothing has been offered to replace it, economists who should know better too often commit the cellophane fallacy by offering a price-increase test as a way of defining a market and indicating the presence or absence of market power in a monopolization case.

The Clinton enforcement agencies could have addressed this vacuum and clarified this murky area. It is disappointing that they did not.[91]

## Conclusion

The Clinton years did embody a more active approach to antitrust enforcement than did the administration's predecessors. But there were important elements of continuity. Further, many of the controversial cases that were initiated during this period had a solid analytical foundation, often based on some variant of the concept of raising rivals' costs. There were disappointments as well. Thus antitrust enforcement during the 1990s is likely to be seen by future generations of analysts as neither one of radical upheaval nor of do-nothing complacency. Instead, it is likely to be

89. Benston (1982); Fisher and McGowan (1983).

90. To return to the Staples–Office Depot merger, the data showed that prices for office products sold by office supply stores were higher in metropolitan areas where only a single chain store was present. Thus one could infer that chain stores in metropolitan areas were a relevant market not only for merger analysis but also for monopoly analysis, and that a single large store in a metropolitan area was exercising market power.

91. For a specific proposal see Nelson and White (2003).

considered an era in which some important initiatives were taken and foundations laid, but also a time when significant opportunities were missed.

## References

Areeda, Philip, and Donald F. Turner. 1975. "Predatory Pricing and Related Practices under Section 2 of the Sherman Act." *Harvard Law Review* 88 (February): 697–733.

Bain, Joe S. 1956. *Barriers to New Competition.* Harvard University Press.

Baker, Jonathan B. 1999. "Econometric Analysis in *FTC* v. *Staples.*" *Journal of Public Policy & Marketing* 18 (Spring): 11–21.

———. 2004. "Efficiencies and High Concentration: Heinz Proposes to Acquire Beech-Nut (2001)." In *The Antitrust Revolution: Economics, Competition, and Policy,* 4th ed., edited by John E. Kwoka Jr. and Lawrence J. White, 150–69. Oxford University Press.

Balto, David A. 1999. "Antitrust Enforcement in the Clinton Administration." *Cornell Journal of Law & Public Policy* 9 (Winter ): 61–134.

Bamberger, Gustavo E. 2004. "Revisiting Maximum Resale Price Maintenance: *State Oil* v. *Khan* (1997)." In *The Antitrust Revolution: Economics, Competition, and Policy,* 4th ed., edited by John E. Kwoka Jr. and Lawrence J. White, 334–49. Oxford University Press.

Baxter, William F. 1980. "The Political Economy of Antitrust." In *The Political Economy of Antitrust: Principal Paper by William Baxter,* edited by Robert D. Tollison, 3–49. D. C. Heath.

Benston, George J. 1982. "Accounting Numbers and Economic Values." *Antitrust Bulletin* 27 (Spring): 161–215.

Bork, Robert H. 1978. *The Antitrust Paradox: A Policy at War with Itself.* Basic Books.

Brennan, Timothy J. 2001."Do Easy Cases Make Bad Law? Antitrust Innovations or Missed Opportunities in *United States* v. *Microsoft.*" *George Washington University Law Review* 69 (October/December): 1042–102.

Brenner, Steven R. 2004. "Potential Competition in Local Telephone Service: Bell Atlantic-NYNEX (1997)." In *The Antitrust Revolution: Economics, Competition, and Policy,* 4th ed., edited by John E. Kwoka Jr. and Lawrence J. White, 73–100. Oxford University Press.

Calkins, Stephen. 2000. "*California Dental Association*: Not a Quick Look but Not the Full Monty." *Antitrust Law Journal* 67 (3): 495–557.

Carlton, Dennis W., and Hal S. Sider. 1999. "Market Power and Vertical Restraints in Retailing Private and an Analysis of *FTC* v. *Toys 'R' Us.*" In *The Role of the Academic Economist in Litigation Support,* edited by Daniel J. Slottje, 67–96. North-Holland.

Dalkir, Serdar, and Frederick R. Warren-Boulton. 2004. "Prices, Market Definition, and the Effects of Merger: Staples–Office Depot (1997)." In *The Antitrust Revolution: Economics, Competition, and Policy,* 4th ed., edited by John E. Kwoka Jr. and Lawrence J. White, 52–72. Oxford University Press.

Edlin, Aaron S., and Joseph Farrell. 2004. "The American Airlines Case: A Chance to Clarify Predation Policy (2001)." In *The Antitrust Revolution: Economics, Competition, and Policy,* 4th ed., edited by John E. Kwoka Jr. and Lawrence J. White, 502–27. Oxford University Press.

Eisner, Marc Allen. 1991. *Antitrust and the Triumph of Economics: Institutions, Expertise, and Policy Change.* University of North Carolina Press.

Evans, David S., and others. 2000. *Did Microsoft Harm Consumers? Two Opposing Views.* AEI-Brookings Joint Center for Regulatory Studies.

Fisher, Franklin M., and John J. McGowan. 1983. "On the Misuse of Accounting Rates of Return to Infer Monopoly Profits." *American Economic Review* 73 (March): 82–97.

Gilbert, Richard J. 1999. "Networks, Standards, and the Use of Market Dominance: Microsoft (1995)." In *The Antitrust Revolution: Economics, Competition, and Policy,* 3d ed., edited by John E. Kwoka Jr. and Lawrence J. White, 409–29. Oxford University Press.

Gilbert, Richard J., and Michael L. Katz. 2001. "An Economist's Guide to *U.S. v. Microsoft.*" *Journal of Economic Perspectives,* 15 (Spring): 25–44.

Gilbert, Richard J., and Willard K. Tom. 2001. "Is Innovation King at the Agencies? The Intellectual Property Guidelines Five Years Later." *Antitrust Law Journal* 69 (1): 43–86.

Horvitz, Paul M. 1996. "Efficiency and Antitrust Considerations in Home Banking: The Proposed Microsoft-Intuit Merger." *Antitrust Bulletin* 41 (Summer): 427–46.

Joskow, Paul L., and Roger G. Noll. 1994. "Economic Regulation: Deregulation and Regulatory Reform during the 1980s." In *American Policy in the 1980s,* edited by Martin Feldstein, 367–440. University of Chicago Press.

Joskow, Paul L., and Nancy L. Rose. 1989. "The Effects of Economic Regulation." In *Handbook of Industrial Organization,* vol. 2, edited by Richard Schmalensee and Robert D. Willig, 1449–506. North Holland.

Katz, Michael L. 2002. "Recent Antitrust Enforcement Actions by the U.S. Department of Justice: A Selective Survey of Economic Issues." *Review of Industrial Organization* 21 (December): 373–97.

Kaysen, Carl, and Donald F. Turner. 1959. *Antitrust Policy: An Economic and Legal Analysis.* Harvard University Press.

Klein, Benjamin. 2001. "The Microsoft Case: What Can a Dominant Firm Do to Defend Its Market Position?" *Journal of Economic Perspectives* 15 (Spring ): 45–62.

Kwoka, John E., Jr., and Lawrence J. White, eds. 1989. *The Antitrust Revolution.* HarperCollins.

———. 1994. *The Antitrust Revolution: The Role of Economics,* 2d ed. HarperCollins.

———. 1999. *The Antitrust Revolution: Economics, Competition, and Policy,* 3d ed. Oxford University Press.

———. 2004a. *The Antitrust Revolution: Economics, Competition, and Policy,* 4th ed. Oxford University Press.

———. 2004b. "Manifest Destiny? The Union Pacific and Southern Pacific Railroad Merger (1996)." In *The Antitrust Revolution: Economics, Competition, and Policy,* 4th ed., edited by John E. Kwoka Jr. and Lawrence J. White, 22–57. Oxford University Press.

Litan, Robert E., and Carl Shapiro. 2002. "Antitrust Policy in the Clinton Administration." In *American Economic Policy in the 1990s,* edited by Jeffrey R. Frankel and Peter R. Orszag, 435–85. MIT Press.

Majure, W. Robert. 1996. "Verified Statement," on behalf of the U.S. Department of Justice, June 3, 1996. Mimeo.

Markham, Jesse W. 1952. *Competition in the Rayon Industry.* Harvard University Press.

Muris, Timothy J. 2000. "The Rule of Reason after *California Dental.*" *Antitrust Law Journal* 68 (2): 527–39.

Nelson, Philip B., and Lawrence J. White. 2003. "Market Definition and the Identification of Market Power in Monopolization Cases: A Critique and a Proposal." Stern School of Business, New York University. Mimeo.

Noll, Roger G. 1989. "Economic Perspectives on the Politics of Regulation." In *Handbook of Industrial Organization,* vol. 2, edited by Richard Schmalensee and Robert D. Willig, 1253–87. North Holland.

Ordover, Janusz A., and Robert D. Willig. 1981. "An Economic Definition of Predation: Pricing and Product Innovation." *Yale Law Journal* 91 (November): 8–53.

Ordover, Janusz A., and Robert D. Willig. 1999. "Access and Bundling in High-Technology Markets." In *Competition, Innovation, and the Microsoft Monopoly: Antitrust in the Digital Marketplace,* edited by Jeffrey A. Eisenach and Thomas M. Lenard, 103–28. Kluwer.

Pelcovits, Michael D. 2004. "The Long Distance Industry: One Merger Too Many? MCI WorldCom and Sprint (2000)." In *The Antitrust Revolution: Economics, Competition, and Policy,* 4th ed., edited by John E. Kwoka Jr. and Lawrence J. White, 101–27. Oxford University Press.

Pitofsky, Robert. 2002a. "Antitrust at the Turn of the 21st Century: The Matter of Remedies." *Georgetown Law Journal* 91 (November): 169–81.

———. 2002b. "Antitrust at the Turn of the 21st Century: A View from the Middle." *St. John's Law Review* 76 (Summer): 583–94.

Posner, Richard A. 1976. *Antitrust Law: An Economic Perspective.* University of Chicago Press.

Priest, George L., and Benjamin Klein. 1984. "The Selection of Disputes for Litigation." *Journal of Legal Studies* 13 (January): 1–55.

Rubinfeld, Daniel L. 2004. "Maintenance of Monopoly: *U.S. v. Microsoft.*" In *The Antitrust Revolution: Economics, Competition, and Policy,* 4th ed., edited by John E. Kwoka Jr. and Lawrence J. White, 476–501. Oxford University Press.

Salop, Steven C., and David T. Scheffman. 1983. "Raising Rivals' Costs." *American Economic Review* 73 (May): 267–71.

———. 1987. "Cost-Raising Strategies." *Journal of Industrial Economics* 36 (September): 19–34.

Salop, Steven C., and Lawrence J. White. 1986. "Economic Analysis of Private Antitrust Litigation." *Georgetown Law Journal* 74 (April): 201–63.

———. 1988. "Private Antitrust Litigation: An Introduction and Framework." In *Antitrust Litigation: New Evidence, New Learning,* edited by Lawrence J. White, 3–60. MIT Press.

Scherer, F. M. 2004. "Retailer-Instigated Restraints on Suppliers' Sales: The Toys 'R' Us Case (2000)." In *The Antitrust Revolution: Economics, Competition, and Policy,* 4th ed., edited by John E. Kwoka Jr. and Lawrence J. White, 373–82. Oxford University Press.

Shapiro, Carl. 2004. "Technology Cross-Licensing Practices: *FTC* v. *Intel* (1999)." In *The Antitrust Revolution: Economics, Competition, and Policy,* 4th ed., edited by John E. Kwoka Jr. and Lawrence J. White, 350–72. Oxford University Press.

Stocking, George W., and Willard F. Mueller. 1955. "The Cellophane Case and the New Competition." *American Economic Review* 45 (March ): 29–63.

Telser, Lester G. 1960. "Why Should Manufacturers Want Fair Trade?" *Journal of Law & Economics* 3 (October): 86–105.

U.S. Department of Justice, Antitrust Division. 1985. "Vertical Restraints Guidelines." Reprinted in *Trade Regulation Report 5*, sec. 5473. Commerce Clearing House.

———. 1998. "Comments of the United States Department of Justice before the Securities and Exchange Commission" (March 6).

Werden, Gregory J. 2000. "Market Delineation under the Merger Guidelines: Monopoly Cases and Alternative Approaches." *Review of Industrial Organization* 16 (March): 211–18.

Whinston, Michael D. 2001. "Exclusivity and Tying in *U.S.* v. *Microsoft*: What We Know and Don't Know." *Journal of Economic Perspectives* 15 (Spring): 63–80.

White, Lawrence J. 1981a. *Reforming Regulation: Processes and Problems*. Prentice-Hall.

———. 1981b. "Vertical Restraints in Antitrust Law: A Coherent Model." *Antitrust Bulletin* 26 (Summer): 327–45.

———. 1988. "Litigation and Economic Incentives." In *Research in Law and Economics*, vol. 11, edited by Richard O. Zerbe, 73–90. JAI Press.

———. 1989. "The Revolution in Antitrust Analysis of Vertical Relationships: How Did We Get from There to Here?" In *Economics and Antitrust Policy*, edited by Robert J. Larner and James W. Meehan, 103–21. Quorum.

———. 1994. "Antitrust vs. Microsoft: Who Won?" *SternBusiness* 1 (Fall): 30–37.

———. 1999. "Wanted: A Market Definition Paradigm for Monopolization Cases." *Computer Industry* 4 (Spring): 1–5.

———. 2000. "Present at the Beginning of a New Era for Antitrust: Reflections on 1982–1983." *Review of Industrial Organization* 16 (March): 131–49.

———. 2001. "A $10 Billion Solution to the Microsoft Problem." *UWLA Law Review* 32 (Symposium): 69–80.

———. 2002a. "The Credit Rating Industry: An Industrial Organization Analysis." In *Ratings, Rating Agencies, and the Global Financial System*, edited by Richard M. Levich, Carmen Reinhart, and Giovanni Majnoni, 41–63. Kluwer.

———. 2002b. "*Staples–Office Depot* and *UP-SP*: An Antitrust Tale of Two Proposed Mergers." In *Measuring Market Power*, edited by Daniel J. Slottje, 150–74. North-Holland.

Williamson, Oliver E. 1968. "Economies as an Antitrust Defense: The Welfare Tradeoffs." *American Economic Review* 58 (March): 18–36.

Winston, Clifford. 1993. "Economic Deregulation: Days of Reckoning for Micro-economists." *Journal of Economic Literature* 31 (September): 1263–89.

ROBERT BORK

# 3 | *High-Stakes Antitrust: The Last Hurrah?*

Though the title of this chapter addresses a question frequently asked as the Bush administration succeeds the Clinton years, there seems no particular reason to believe that we have seen the last of high-stakes antitrust cases, to be followed, one supposes, by run-of-the-mill price-fixing prosecutions. There is, to be sure, something to be said for such a development. Too often the government has brought misguided high-stakes actions without first asking whether a company's domination of its market was due to superior efficiency or to tactics serving no purpose other than to suppress competition by injuring or destroying competitors. The seemingly interminable prosecution of IBM is, of course, a case in point, as was the long preparation of the Justice Department's Antitrust Division, on no intelligible theory, to cut General Motors down to a size the division preferred. That ambition was thwarted when Japanese automakers got there first, accomplishing by competition what the division wanted to do by judicial fiat. Competition, which reflected the balance of consumers' preferences, was of course a far better solution than the guesses of judges guided by the guesses of battalions of lawyers.

Antitrust policy in both government enforcement and judicial understanding has greatly improved since those benighted years, although the antitrust adventures and calamities of that era should be borne in mind, for they counsel caution in applying law today to alter market outcomes. Still, there remain large and complex cases in which law should intervene to remedy private behavior that stifles the market. Two of the three cases discussed in this chapter fit that description.

The government's antitrust cases against Microsoft, Visa and Master-Card, and American Airlines are surely not the last of the behemoths, and they illustrate both the best and the worst of antitrust enforcement.[1] It may be that the Bush administration has less appetite for such high-stakes antitrust actions than its predecessor had, a supposition supported by the administration's haste to drop the Microsoft case through a settlement that gives back much of what had been won in the courts. But enthusiasm for antitrust waxes and wanes; sooner or later, big cases will be back, and the best of them will be justified by sound economic analysis.

It is often misleading, in any event, to compare administrations as though they followed coherent antitrust policies dictated by the White House. Sometimes the White House orders dispositions of particular cases, but much often depends on the independent views of the Antitrust Division. My own impression is that the three cases referred to here as high-stakes had less to do with any overall strategy of the Clinton administration than with the views of Assistant Attorney General Joel Klein.

Much of the conservative indignation over these cases arose from little more than the fact that they were initiated by a Clinton appointee, or in some cases from a reflexive antipathy to any antitrust enforcement. The merits of the cases should be judged, however, not on ideological moods but on their soundness in law and economics. From that perspective, two of the three seem solidly grounded. What legitimate purpose the government hoped to achieve by the third, that against American Airlines, remains something of a mystery.

All three cases involve network industries that appear likely to be increasingly a concern of antitrust enforcement, although it is not clear that the existence of a network should be grounds for suspicion in itself. The court of appeals' *Microsoft* opinion summarized the network problem: "In markets characterized by network effects, one product or standard tends toward dominance, because 'the utility that a user derives from consumption of the good increases with the number of other agents consuming the good.'" The classic example, of course, is the telephone market. The more households and businesses that subscribe to a telephone com-

---

1. I had a small part in each of these, consulting with or representing companies favoring the cases against Microsoft and Visa/MasterCard and with the defendant American Airlines.

pany's services, the more valuable the telephone to each subscriber. Quoting an economist, the court said, "Once a product or standard achieves wide acceptance, it becomes more or less entrenched. Competition in such industries is 'for the field' rather than 'within the field.'"[2]

Networks, then, seem to be a form of efficiency; that is, they are valuable to consumers. They also make life more difficult for rivals, but efficiencies do that; indeed, for antitrust purposes, pleasing consumers is efficiency. It is not entirely the case, moreover, that the presence of a widely accepted network produces such a deep entrenchment that competition in the industry is for the field rather than within the field.

An examination of these cases suggests just that: network efficiencies are by no means invariably so powerful that they suppress competition. Thus in two of the three cases, *Microsoft* and *Visa/MasterCard*, the network defendants found it necessary or at least advisable to resort to illegal behavior to ensure their continued dominance of their markets. In the third, *American Airlines*, there was competition from numerous competing networks, both national and regional, and point-to-point carriers. Antitrust and enforcement agencies may be in danger of seeing too much significance in the existence of networks. Perhaps those agencies and the courts should focus almost entirely on the presence or absence of nonefficient exclusionary tactics. Where a network is so powerful that it confers a natural monopoly, the alternatives should not include antitrust prosecution but a choice between governmental abstention and regulation.

## The Microsoft Case

*Microsoft* is one of the most extraordinary cases in the annals of antitrust actions. It was one of the very few cases in which successful predation by a monopolist was proved. A unanimous en banc court of appeals in an extraordinarily comprehensive opinion upheld the finding of predation and clarified the law in important respects. Despite the government's victory, however, the Bush administration has attempted to surrender the victories the Clinton administration won in the courts. It is too early to say whether the courts will permit that capitulation.

This case was only the latest attempt to require Microsoft to abide by the antitrust laws. The United States sued in 1994 to prevent the company

---

2. *United States* v. *Microsoft*, 253 F.3d 34, 49 (D.C. Cir. 2001).

from employing anticompetitive tactics to maintain its monopoly in the market for personal computer operating system software. The case was settled by consent decree in 1995. The decree contained a provision that forbade operating system license agreements conditioned on precluding the licensing of any other product but said that Microsoft was not prohibited from developing integrated products.[3] This introduced an ambiguity. Was incorporating the browser into the operating system a forbidden conditioning or an allowable integration? In an enforcement action brought by the government three years later, a three-judge panel of the Court of Appeals for the District of Columbia Circuit Court held that the technological bundling of Microsoft's browser, the Internet Explorer, with its operating system, Windows, did not violate the consent decree, but the court reserved the question of whether that bundling might violate sections 1 or 2 of the Sherman Anti-Trust Act.[4]

Shortly before the decision was issued, the Justice Department and a group of state plaintiffs filed separate complaints, which were then consolidated, alleging four violations of the Sherman Act: exclusive dealing arrangements and tying the Internet Explorer to Windows, both in violation of section 1; and maintenance of the operating system monopoly by unlawful means and attempted monopolization of the Internet browser market, both in violation of section 2. The primary focus of the case was Microsoft's alleged use of these tactics to eliminate the Netscape Navigator and Sun Microsystems' Java as threats to Microsoft's operating system monopoly. The court of appeals affirmed the district court's judgment that Microsoft violated section 2 in maintaining its monopoly in the operating system market. But it reversed the judgment that Microsoft illegally attempted to monopolize the browser market, and it remanded to the district court the finding that tying the browser to the operating system violated section 1. The core of the decision was that the company monopolized the operating system market. I will focus primarily on that.

Quoting the Supreme Court, the court of appeals observed that the offense of monopolization has two elements: "(1) the possession of monopoly power in the relevant market and (2) the willful acquisition or maintenance of that power as distinguished by growth or development as a consequence of a superior product, business acumen, or historic accident."[5]

---

3. *United States* v. *Microsoft*, 56 F.3d 1448 (D.C. Cir. 1995).

4. *United States* v. *Grinnell Corp*, 384 U.S. 563, 570–71 (1966), quoted in *United States* v. *Microsoft*, 147 F.3d 935 (D.C. Cir. 1998).

5. *United States* v. *Microsoft*, 253 F.3d, 34, 50 (D.C. Cir. 1998).

Thus it is not per se a violation of section 2 to destroy a rival. Destruction by superior efficiency must be allowable if the economy is to be vigorous and serve consumer welfare. The law uses the "predation" for the employment of tactics that eliminate or marginalize competitors by means other than efficiency. Though examples of predation are more rare than the law once imagined, they do exist, and Microsoft's campaign to defend its monopoly in the operating system market is one such example.

Microsoft and some of its apologists derided the government's case as resting upon a theory of "predatory innovation," but that is a false characterization. The gravamen of the complaint was that Microsoft's integration of its operating system and browser produced no efficiencies, innovative or otherwise, but was designed solely to drive Netscape's browser from the market. Microsoft's browser did not become superior to Netscape's until the predatory campaign so reduced Netscape's revenue that it was incapable of keeping up in research and development.

Although the court of appeals did not cite them all, Microsoft's internal communications amply demonstrate that the company intended to engage in predatory warfare that had nothing to do with achieving greater efficiency. This documentary evidence related primarily to the company's desire to eliminate a competitive browser that had the potential of performing functions that would undercut the monopoly by overcoming the applications barrier. That barrier arises from two related factors. Consumers prefer an operating system for which a large number of applications have already been written, and most developers of applications prefer to write for an operating system that already has a substantial customer base. Microsoft had more than 70,000 applications written for Explorer, and the company controlled a 95 percent share of consumers in its market. To succeed, an entrant into the operating system market would have to perform the probably impossible task of simultaneously attracting enough applications written for it to attract consumers and enough consumers to make it worthwhile for applications developers to write for the new operating system.

It was this formidable applications barrier that the Netscape Navigator and Sun Microsystems' Java technology, singly or in combination, threatened to breach. The Navigator, which complemented the operating system, might evolve to receive applications, while Java is a "language" that could run on most or all operating systems. Either or both together could make applications developers and consumers indifferent to what operating system underlay them. The market would be open for competitive systems.

Microsoft saw the danger at once. Bill Gates wrote that Netscape's strategy was to "commoditize the underlying operating system," which meant that operating systems would become fungible and would command only a competitive rate of return. Other Microsoft executives were equally explicit, commenting that the company's operating system was threatened at a "fundamental level," that "Netscape/Java is using the browser to create a 'virtual operating system,'" and that a competing browser could eventually "obsolete Windows."[6]

Microsoft's response was to develop the Internet Explorer and force it upon distributors and computer manufacturers. The primary strategy was to commingle the code for its browser and operating system so that computer manufacturers (original equipment manufacturers, or OEMs) and computer purchasers were required to take the Explorer, which was added without charge. This forced Netscape to stop charging for the Navigator and start giving it away, a defensive maneuver that could not last long. As Steve Ballmer, the number two man at Microsoft, stated: "We're giving away a pretty good browser as part of the operating system. How long can [Netscape] survive selling it?"[7] He added that Microsoft had to expand into Netscape's territory lest Netscape encroach on his operating system territory.

Other senior Microsoft officials were, if anything, even more explicit that incorporation of the browser into the operating system had nothing to do with increasing efficiency but only with attacking the Navigator. One wrote, "It seems clear that it will be very hard to increase browser market share on the merits of [the Internet Explorer] alone. It will be more important to leverage the [operating system] asset to make people use IE instead of Navigator." Another wrote, "I thought our #1 strategic imperative was to get IE share—they've been stalled and their best hope is tying tight to Windows, esp. on OEM machines." Microsoft concluded that if Windows and the Internet Explorer "are decoupled then Navigator has a good chance of winning" and that "if we take away IE for the [operating system], most nav users will never switch to us."[8] Microsoft Senior Vice President James Allchin wrote that "leveraging Windows from a marketing perspective"

6. These comments, taken from Microsoft's internal documents, are reprinted in the "Memorandum of the United States in Support of Motion for Preliminary Injunction" ("U.S. Memo") filed in the Justice Department's Sherman Act case against Microsoft. The documents themselves are filed under seal with the court. These quotations appear on page 21 of the memo.

7. Jeffrey Young, "The George S. Patton of Software," *Forbes*, January 27, 1997, pp. 86, 88.

8. "U.S. Memo," p. 10; "Complaint" in *United States* v. *Microsoft Corp.* ("U.S. Complaint"), Civ. Action No. 98-5012, para. 114d.

was necessary if the Explorer were to defeat the Navigator. "I am convinced we have to use Windows—this is the one thing they don't have. . . . We have to be competitive with features, but we need something more—Windows integration." He stated further that "Memphis [the code name for Windows 98] must be a simple upgrade, but most importantly it must be a killer on OEM so that Netscape never gets a chance on these systems."[9]

Reliance on blustering documents to establish an antitrust case is usually misleading. Every antitrust lawyer knows that businessmen often use the language of professional football or war: "We are going to crush our competitors," "We'll chop them into little bloody bits," or similarly endearing phrases. These are usually mere manifestations of the aggressive spirit appropriate to competitive markets. But Microsoft's language is different in kind: it not only states its intent to win but outlines the tactics it intends to use, tactics that have nothing to do with competing on the merits or triumphing by superior efficiency. Rather, these statements set forth a strategy for suppressing nascent competition through a technique that excludes rivals without advancing consumer welfare. If that strategy proved successful, consumers would be damaged through maintenance of monopoly prices and the loss of competing sources of innovation. The strategy was, in fact, followed, and the result was, as predicted, the destruction of Netscape's Navigator.

Microsoft buttressed the effect of bundling its browser and operating system by entering into exclusive dealing contracts with Internet access providers (IAPs) and Internet service vendors (ISVs), contracts for which it was unable at trial to offer any procompetitive justifications. Computer manufacturers and access providers were by far the largest channels of distribution for browsers, but the contracts with service vendors foreclosed additional channels, and all three arrangements were held to violate section 2 of the Sherman Act.

Similarly illegal were Microsoft's dealings with Apple, which had its own operating system but installed the Netscape Navigator. Apple was vulnerable because it used Microsoft's Office, a suite of business productivity applications that was used by 90 percent of Macintosh operating system users running such a suite. Apple's business was in steep decline, and had Microsoft announced it was ceasing to develop new versions of Macintosh Office, a great part of the industry would have regarded the announcement as Apple's death notice. Microsoft used that probability to force

9. "U.S. Memo," pp. 10–11; "U.S. Complaint," para. 114c.

Apple to stop installing Navigator and switch to Explorer. Bill Gates said, "I think . . . Apple should be using [Internet Explorer] everywhere and if they don't do it, then we can use Office as a club."[10] It was so used, and Apple capitulated.

The court of appeals upheld the district court's definition of the relevant market as the licensing of all Intel-compatible personal computer operating systems worldwide. That definition resulted in a market share greater than 95 percent. If the Macintosh operating system were included, Microsoft's share of the market would be greater than 80 percent. Both percentages are sufficient to establish monopoly power unless easy market entry negated such power. Microsoft's objections to that market definition and the finding of monopoly power were readily disposed of since it could not establish that the district court's findings of fact were clearly erroneous.

Quite aside from that, however, a consideration not mentioned by either the district court or the court of appeals demonstrates the correctness of the market definition and the finding of monopoly power. Microsoft employed tactics that were designed to be and were effective in excluding competition, and it could not show any competitive justification for those tactics, such as achieving greater efficiency. The company itself defined the market by the companies it attacked. No predator would attack particular firms if other firms, unaffected by the onslaught, remained to offer competition. The argument is analogous to that defining the market in a price-fixing conspiracy. When the conspiracy is proved, per se illegality follows; no defense of lack of market power will be entertained. Nobody fixes prices without power in the market; that would be futile, since it would cause a collapse of the conspirators' sales. Similarly, no predator incurs the high cost of attacking one or two rivals if other rivals remain to prevent the predator from achieving or maintaining monopoly power.

Sun's Java, a set of technologies, is another type of middleware that created a potential threat to the Windows monopoly. Programs calling upon Java application programming interfaces (APIs) would run on any operating system with a set of programs written in the Java programming language and a Java Virtual Machine (JVM) that translates byte code into instructions to the operating system. Since Java, like the Netscape Navigator, would work with any operating system, it too posed a threat to Microsoft's operating system monopoly. With the Navigator and Java APIs avail-

10. *Microsoft*, 253 F3d, 73.

able, application writers might no longer be confined to writing for Microsoft's Windows, and consumers could get all the applications they wanted using any operating system. Microsoft therefore anticipated the possible erosion of its monopoly.

Microsoft took a license from Sun but then designed a JVM incompatible with Sun's so that it was difficult or impossible to use applications written for one on the other. Microsoft made exclusive deals with the leading Internet server vendors that, as the court put it, "took place against a backdrop of foreclosure."[11] Netscape announced it would include with every copy of Navigator a copy of Windows JVM that complied with Sun's standards, giving Sun's Java the necessary presence on Windows; thus Microsoft's foreclosure of the distribution of Navigator seriously damaged the distribution of Sun's JVM. The exclusive dealing agreements with the vendors also foreclosed a substantial portion of the field for JVM distribution, protected Microsoft's monopoly from a middleware threat, and once again did so without procompetitive justification.

Microsoft further impeded the growth of cross-platform Java by pressuring Intel to stop developing a high-performance Windows-compatible JVM that would endanger the company's monopoly in the operating systems market. Microsoft threatened that if Intel did not stop aiding Sun, Microsoft would refuse to distribute Intel technologies bundled with Windows. The final blow was administered when an Intel competitor sought support from Microsoft and the company informed Intel that it would not support that competitor if Intel would stop working on Java. Intel surrendered.

Microsoft's crowning act of commercial thuggery, however, entailed outright fraud. The company created a set of software development tools to assist Internet server vendors in designing Java applications. These tools were incompatible with Sun's goal of achieving cross-platform uses for Java, but Microsoft told developers that the tools were compatible. The intended result was that developers unknowingly wrote applications software that would work only with Windows. As a Microsoft internal memorandum said, the goal was to "kill cross-platform Java by grow[ing] the polluted Java market."[12]

There is much more in the court of appeals' opinion, but this recitation is sufficient to support the conclusion that Microsoft employed

11. *Microsoft*, 253 F.3d, 75.
12. *Microsoft*, 253 F.3d, 76–77.

anticompetitive tactics in violation of section 2 of the Sherman Act to maintain its monopoly.

Two further matters deserve mention: the argument about network effects and the reason why predation was possible here although properly viewed with suspicion when alleged in most cases. First, Microsoft is engaged in a dynamic technological market characterized by network effects. The more developers wrote applications for Windows, the more valuable Windows became to each of them by attracting more consumers. The applications barrier inherent in that situation may be seen as the result of the superior efficiency of the network, but that argument falls short of justifying the company's conduct. Microsoft had indeed achieved dominance and entrenchment. New operating systems could not breach the applications barrier. That did not mean, however, that new technologies might not render Windows less potent by circumventing the barrier. When the Navigator and Java threatened to do just that, Microsoft feared it could not rely on the entrenchment inherent in its network and instead resorted to predation to destroy the incipient competition it perceived. Whatever answer an antitrust action might devise for monopolies protected by network effects, there is no reason whatever to allow those effects to be supplemented by deliberate exclusionary tactics having no procompetitive justifications. Competition for the field deserves protection every bit as much as competition within the field.

Second, commentators have long been suspicious of claims of predation by price cutting. Such predation is extremely unlikely to succeed and, if in some conceivable case it should, the predator would almost never be able to recoup the losses incurred in the warfare. Microsoft's campaign resembled price-cutting predation in that it gave price and other concessions (translatable into price) to those vendors it demanded stop dealing with Netscape and Sun, and it also had to increase its output of browsers and JVMs. For that reason, I have been asked whether my conclusion that Microsoft was guilty of unlawful predation is consistent with my previous conclusions in *The Antitrust Paradox*. Though I did not foresee a case quite like *Microsoft*, I identified the kind of case in which predation would be profitable, and *Microsoft* fits into that category.

After arguing, at greater length than I have here, that cases of predatory price cutting are rare to nonexistent, I concluded that the analysis "also indicates that we should look for methods of predation which do not require the predator to expand output and incur disproportionately large costs." I then argued that predation through the misuse of governmental processes was such a technique. Predators have, for example, engaged in sham litigation that imposes equal costs on the predator and the victim. "Expenses in complex business litigation can be enormous, not merely in direct legal costs and fees but in diversion of executive effort and disruption of the business organization's activities. Where the object of predatory litigation is to drive an existing rival from a market altogether, the technique will generally be useful only by a larger firm against a smaller, since equal absolute costs will be proportionally greater for the smaller firm."[13]

This rationale fits *Microsoft*. The company did not increase output to drive the price of browsers down; the increase was the intended result of the predatory tactics and did not entail any increase in the company's marginal costs. The costs associated with a software code lie in research and development. Once the code exists, the costs of distribution (marginal costs) do not rise significantly with increases in the amounts distributed. The predator is not penalized by the increase in production. Even when Microsoft distributed its browser free, it simply sacrificed fixed costs and forced Netscape to do the same. Microsoft's reserves were more than ninety times larger than Netscape's: the market capitalization of Microsoft was approximately $250 billion while Netscape's was $2.7 billion. In addition, Microsoft was defending monopoly profits that made the expense of predation worthwhile. Even after the sacrificed fixed costs of developing the Internet Explorer, the company was earning supracompetitive returns on the monopoly it was defending, while Netscape, forced to distribute its Navigator free, had no income in that market to cover its fixed costs. Understandably, Netscape gave up a contest it could not win. This technique of predation belongs in the same category as sham litigation.

It is to be expected that cases similar in principle to *Microsoft* will occur in the future. Other markets are occupied by network firms, and increasingly rapid technological change will undoubtedly threaten their monopoly positions. If they respond as Microsoft did, antitrust cases are likely to be brought. Indeed, Microsoft itself may be a candidate for further antitrust action because it appears not to have changed its behavior. The consent decree it entered with the government—and that a new district judge approved as required by the Tunney Act—is essentially meaningless: it does not even prohibit the behavior the district court and the en banc court of appeals held illegal. There is, for instance, no restriction on the commingling of code that bolted together the Windows operating system

13. Bork (1993, pp. 155, 159).

and the Internet Explorer. As far as the decree is concerned, Microsoft can do to other rivals precisely what it did to Netscape.

## The Visa and MasterCard Cases

The case against Visa and MasterCard was, if not quite a slam dunk, close to it. The Visa and MasterCard networks are owned by their member banks, and because each has signed up virtually every bank in the United States, the same banks own both of them. The relevant markets were the general-purpose network services and the general-purpose card market. Together Visa and MasterCard member banks issue 85 percent of all general-purpose cards.

A Visa bylaw provided that "the membership of any member shall automatically terminate in the event it . . . issues . . . Discover Cards or American Express Cards, or any other card deemed competitive by the Board of Directors."[14] When MasterCard learned that four or five major banks were considering issuing American Express cards, it adopted a competitive programs policy (CPP) that had the same effect as the Visa bylaws. The Visa board never "deemed competitive" the cards issued by Master-Card member banks or banks that issued cards for Diners Club, owned by Citibank, a member of both Visa and MasterCard. MasterCard similarly overlooked banks that issued the competing Visa and Diners Club cards.

The legal framework governing the case is clear. Not many years ago these arrangements would have been held illegal per se under section 1 of the Sherman Act, which prohibits combinations and conspiracies in restraint of trade. That rule made no economic sense and was inconsistently applied. The agreement among the banks not to deal with American Express, Discover, or any other card issuer "deemed competitive" was a horizontal agreement not to compete by offering the cards of those issuers. That is, it was an agreement not to compete between entities capable of competing—a horizontal restraint. A rule of law making such agreements illegal per se would, if consistently enforced, outlaw most joint ventures, including law firms (which typically have rules against any member taking business in competition with the firm).

The new legal rule, followed by the district court, is that entities capable of competing with one another may combine their skills to operate

---

14. *United States* v. *Visa U.S.A. Inc.*, 163 F. Supp.2d. 322, 379 (S.D.N.Y. 2001).

more efficiently and may employ reasonable restraints on their competition with one another to increase that efficiency. Once a plaintiff shows the existence of an agreement restraining competition, the burden shifts to the defendant joint venture to prove a valid business justification, the creation of efficiencies. The Visa bylaw and MasterCard's competitive programs policy were on their face agreed eliminations of competition at the level of card issuance by banks. The agreements also threatened the vigor of network rivalry among Visa, MasterCard, American Express, and Discover.

The first effect was obvious: banks could not compete with one another by offering American Express or Discover cards. Some banks wanted to offer those cards. When the MasterCard board was considering adopting the competitive programs policy, six board members objected on the grounds that the market should decide what was offered and that banks, like supermarkets, should be able to offer customers all brands. These banks clearly saw that consumer choice was being narrowed, a matter of importance because the networks offered different features that appealed to various groups of cardholders.

Even after Visa and MasterCard imposed restraints, some banks wanted to offer American Express and Discover and pulled back only when they considered the likelihood of losing Visa and MasterCard membership. A bank that lost those memberships would experience significant customer disruption and would be forced to liquidate or sell existing Visa and MasterCard customer accounts, lose access to the Plus and Cirrus ATM networks, and give up the extensive merchant acceptance of Visa and MasterCard. Every bank that considered these costs decided not to offer American Express and Discover cards.

The effect of the restraints upon competition at the network level was perhaps even more important. When multiple banks issue general-purpose cards, networks are strengthened in three fundamental ways: increased numbers of cards issued, increased merchant acceptance, and increased economies of scale. The court said that although there were thousands of issuers already in the United States, more is always better for card issuance. When more merchants accept the cards, more cards are issued. American Express, for example, had not been able to attract a significant number of small merchants, and that situation would not improve until the merchants saw more consumers with American Express cards. Economies of scale drive the card network business by lowering network costs and allowing networks to offer services at lower prices, a saving passed on to consumers.

The court elaborated on the crucial importance of multiple bank issuers to a card network. American Express and Discover could not duplicate the strength and breadth of coverage and acceptance by thousands of different entities. Banks, moreover, offer cross-selling opportunities to more profitable steady customers, those who already have a checking or savings account or other relationship. This became of greater importance as direct mail responses dwindled from 5 or 3 percent to 1 percent. Branch bank solicitations are also less expensive for issuers than direct mail solicitations, and steady customers are more profitable than others because banks already have better credit information on them and suffer fewer defaults.

In addition, banks provide networks with links to customers' checking accounts, which is crucial because debit cards instantaneously pay for a transaction by debiting the cardholder's account. In addition, debit cards will be the bridge to new multifunction chip cards, which will offer both credit and debit services among other features. Being unable to deal with banks belonging to Visa and MasterCard, American Express and Discover have no access to any customer's checking account and so are handicapped in offering debit cards and multifunction chip cards. The chip card is dependent on applications developers, thus creating a chicken-and-egg problem like that posed by Microsoft: software developers have little or no incentive to write applications for cards that do not have wide distribution.

American Express and Discover, were they not excluded, have much to offer banks besides a choice of card features. They are both closed-loop systems that deal directly with merchants and consequently have developed infrastructures to collect data about spending that are considered superior to Visa's and MasterCard's capabilities. This allows promotions targeted to various consumer segments. The banks in turn have experience and expertise in innovating and marketing card features that would be valuable to American Express and Discover. The combination of the strengths of those networks and the banks would, of course, be valuable to consumers.

After the government made these showings to the satisfaction of the court, the burden shifted to Visa and MasterCard to offer procompetitive justifications for their restraints. Those they offered were quickly dismissed by the court. For one thing, evidence showed that Visa's and MasterCard's motives were not to increase efficiency but to restrict competition at network and issuer levels. The argument that the restraints promoted loyalty and cohesion was inconsistent with the facts. Both Visa and MasterCard negotiated individual compensation packages with certain banks controlling more than half of all card issuance, and that differential treatment of banks did not cause disruption. In addition, the same banks belonged to both the Visa and MasterCard networks, and that did not compromise cohesion in either network. Citibank was dedicating its efforts to Master-Card, although it was also a member of Visa and controlled Diners Club. That situation had caused no divisiveness or lack of cohesion on the Visa board. There were also no adverse effects outside the United States, where many member banks offer American Express cards.

The argument that if American Express were allowed to deal with banks, it would skim off the best prospects was rebutted with the observation that both Visa and MasterCard engage in the same selective behavior. (In any event such "cherry picking," if indeed it would occur, sounds like competition for the most lucrative customers, hardly a competitive evil.) The argument was also advanced that American Express and Discover would be able to take a free ride on assets developed by Visa and Master-Card. The flaw in that contention was that neither of those companies had any rules concerning member banks' use of their card-issuing relationships, data, and information. This, coupled with testimony from the banks, Visa, and MasterCard that those networks had no interest in the member banks' relationships with their customers, meant that there was no asset on which free-riding could occur. The district court accordingly held these rules and policies to be violations of section 1 of the Sherman Act.

## Causation and Consumer Harm in *Microsoft* and *Visa/MasterCard*

The chapter by Howard H. Chang, David S. Evans, and Richard Schmalensee, "Has the Consumer Harm Standard Lost Its Teeth?," finds the government's approach to the issue of causation in both *Microsoft* and *Visa/MasterCard* seriously deficient. I believe the authors do so under a false impression of what the government argued and what the courts decided.

The authors pose the issue they address as the important differences between those who insist on direct proof of harm to consumers and those who are willing to infer consumer harm from harm to competitors, thus offering a choice only between the impracticable and the disastrous. If that really were the choice, theirs would certainly be the better one. It would be prudent, to say the least, to allow some predators to roam unhindered rather than to shut down the competitive process altogether.[15] Fortunately, that is not the real choice.

I would rephrase the issue as one between those who insist on direct proof of consumer harm and those who think that consumer harm can be inferred from certain forms of exclusionary market behavior that cannot be shown to create or maintain efficiency. This is the rationale on which *Microsoft* and *Visa/MasterCard* were decided. The authors, however, present a simplified version of the government's position in the two cases: "A canonical view of the Clinton approach based on a review of *Microsoft*, *Visa*, and *Intel*."[16] First, they contend, the government presented evidence to demonstrate that competitors were harmed. Second, it presented evidence to demonstrate that the harmed competitors were important ones (either actual or potential) in concentrated markets, so that harm to competitors constituted harm to competition or to the competitive process. The government believed this was sufficient for a finding of liability because harm to consumers could be inferred from harm to competition or to the competitive process.

Neither the government nor the courts proceeded by so simple-minded a formula. In both cases Antitrust Division lawyers and economists heard repeated presentations from Microsoft and from Visa and MasterCard as well as from competitors that believed they had been harmed by illegal behavior. The potential defendants offered reasons why their behavior was legal and why their behavior had not harmed consumers but rather had conferred benefits upon them. Corporations favoring government prosecution advanced arguments to the contrary.[17] Harm to consumers was a crucial factor in the government's decision to go forward with a case or to refuse to do so.

---

15. It is not clear, however, whether the authors' insistence of direct proof of harm to consumers would not also apply to laws seeking to prevent monopolistic mergers and price-fixing cartels. If that were the case, their prescription would largely, if not entirely, repeal the antitrust laws, which might not qualify as a calamity but would be a needless sacrifice of a body of law that, wisely administered, as it increasingly is, confers real benefits for consumer welfare.

16. *Intel* was a poorly conceived Federal Trade Commission case over which the Clinton administration had no direct control. The case went nowhere and ended in a settlement that accomplished little. As the authors observe, the settlement meant that the publicly available record does not permit discussion in the detail they devote to the other two cases.

17. Then and later the defendants and their supporters emphasized that competitors were urging government action, implying or stating that this emphasis created a taint of illegitimacy to the prosecutions. The truth is that many cases, probably a large majority, are first called to the Antitrust Division's attention by competitors' complaints. The division does not have FBI agents roaming the

The same process occurred in the courts. The government was required to show behavior of the sort that was likely to harm competitors illegitimately and thus cause harm to the competitive process. The defendants attempted to counter that showing. If they had succeeded, the cases would have ended there with judgments for the defendants. And in both cases the government prevailed at this stage. It was then up to the defendants to show that there were valid business justifications for their actions, that the questioned behavior created efficiencies valuable to consumers.

It is entirely proper that the burden of showing efficiencies be placed on the defendants. They have superior knowledge of the reasons for their conduct and its likely effect on consumers. It would be absurd to place on the government the burden of proving the negative, that there were no efficiencies served. Once the defendants advanced their efficiency justifications, the government attempted to counter them. In both cases the defendants failed to carry their burden, and judgment properly went to the government.

This is not at all the way the authors describe what happened. They simply leave out the crucial stage of the proceedings in which the claimed consumer-valuable efficiencies were examined through the presentation of evidence and argument. Only by doing that can they answer in the affirmative the question posed in the title of their chapter: "Has the Consumer Harm Standard Lost Its Teeth?"

Which leads to their second contention, that consumer harm must be proved through direct evidence rather than, as the government and the courts thought, by inference from a showing of the intentional infliction of harm upon competitors without any reason grounded in greater efficiency and consumer welfare. Direct proof of consumer harm is usually impossible or unreliable to collect, but the inference described is wholly reliable.

The authors state their point clearly. "We believe that evidence of likely consumer harm—in the form of substantial deleterious effects on prices, production, or quality—should be required for antitrust liability in rule-of-reason Sherman Act cases. If harm to consumers is difficult to show, that should be a clear signal that any harm to competitors may not have had any significant effect on competition." Harmful effects on price,

---

economy looking for antitrust infractions. Competitors with first-hand knowledge of what is taking place in an industry are the best source of information. The division then undertakes the task of determining whether the complaints are really protests against hard competition that the complainers are losing or whether there is a solid basis in law for their concerns.

quantity, or quality are each restrictions on output, the proper concern of antitrust. The only question is how courts should arrive at a determination that a restriction of output is or is likely to be the result of a questioned action or agreement.

The authors suggest that lack of harm to competition should be inferred from a failure to show harm to consumers by empirical investigation. That Netscape's browser was driven from the market by nonefficient exclusionary practices would be of no concern if there were no direct proof of consumer harm. This is a curious argument. First, the absence of direct proof of consumer harm should be viewed with suspicion because it is abundantly clear that Microsoft, which knew the situation best, intended its actions to preserve a monopoly, and an unnecessary monopoly produces consumer harm. Suppose, however, that Microsoft was mistaken, that Netscape's browser could never have attracted sufficient applications to displace Windows to any significant extent. There was still harm to consumers because a product that many consumers preferred was taken from them.

Finally, assume that Microsoft's attack proved not to be the real reason for the disappearance of the Netscape Navigator. Even then, what harm is done by finding a violation of law? The result would be only an injunction that proved unnecessary against illegal practices. There could be no structural relief, no question of divestiture, because it could not have been shown that Netscape would in fact have succeeded in altering the condition of the market for personal computer operating systems. Microsoft's employment of exclusionary practices that neither create nor express efficiency is utterly without social value and should be enjoined because otherwise they may be, and given what we know of Microsoft's history, will be employed again in this or in its many other markets.

It is no objection to say that such a finding of law violation may be used against Microsoft in private triple-damage actions. If the predator intended to kill a victim to harm consumers, the fact that the victim was killed due to a misapprehension by the predator should surely not be a defense. The attempted murder of an aunt to obtain her estate is not excused because the proximate cause of death was a heart attack. The situations differ only in that in a Sherman Act prosecution for predation, it is necessary to show a monopolizing motive, either directly or by necessary inference from the course of conduct pursued, to distinguish the case from one complaining of a mere commercial tort. In Microsoft's case there was an abundance of both direct and circumstantial proof.

The analysis of *Visa/MasterCard* is very similar to that of *Microsoft*. The agreements of the banks in the two systems not to issue American Express or Discover cards was of a sort familiar to antitrust law: a horizontal agreement among competitors to refuse to deal and thus not to compete by offering new brands to their customers. The facts surrounding the inception of the two agreements made it plain that their objective was to prevent, so far as possible, American Express and Discover from reaching consumers. Nor is there any doubt that the agreements did just that. The authors, however, insist that the government should have provided evidence of the extent to which American Express and Discover were harmed, evidence from projections of the growth of cards issued and the like. This is an idle argument. When a competitor is blocked from avenues of distribution by a horizontal agreement not to compete, an exclusionary practice has been identified.[18]

That much having been shown, the burden of persuasion shifted to Visa and MasterCard to show the efficiencies created or maintained (and thus the economic benefits to consumers) by the agreements.[19] This the defendants signally failed to do. The authors advance arguments rejected at trial and shown to be false by the experience in countries that disapproved of the exclusionary agreements because the absence of such agreements inflicted no inefficiencies on Visa and MasterCard. It is similarly a red herring to say that exclusive dealing agreements (such as United Airlines' agreement to serve only Pepsi-owned soft drinks on its flights) are legal.

18. The authors state that "if an excluded manufacturer were unable to distribute its products effectively, depriving consumers of the ability to choose its products, that might constitute significant consumer harm. In this case the evidence indicated that American Express could reach all consumers." American Express could do so only by direct mail advertising, and the evidence showed that the effectiveness of that avenue of distribution was weak and deteriorating. The argument is similar to Microsoft's that computer users could download the Netscape Navigator from the Internet. That could have been done, but it was a cumbersome and inconvenient process that offered no real alternative to distribution through original equipment manufacturers, Internet server vendors, and Internet access providers.

19. This involves the now familiar distinction between ancillary and naked restraints of trade. An ancillary and therefore lawful agreement not to compete is one that accompanies and makes more efficient the integration of some economic activities of otherwise independent actors. I have used the web of agreements not to compete on hourly rates and on divisions of fields of activity characteristic of law firms as an example of ancillary and lawful agreements to suppress competition within the unit. Where there is no integration of the economic activities of separate persons or firms, an agreement not to compete is a naked restraint and unlawful. Some such agreements—a price-fixing cartel, for example—are classified as per se illegal. Others, where the relationship of the agreement to economic efficiency is not immediately apparent, are examined under the quick-look procedure or a more extensive rule-of-reason inquiry.

Coca-Cola and other companies are free to compete for such contracts and, the decisive point, there was no agreement among United, American, Delta, Northwest, Continental, Southwest, and the other airlines not to sell Coke or anything but Pepsi. Had there been, the government would have been interested to hear what consumer-valuable efficiencies flowed from such an agreement.

In short, when a monopolist or a group of competitors having monopoly power acting in unison employs exclusionary tactics, it is relevant to ask why they did it. If no valid business justifications (efficiency justifications) are forthcoming, it is fair to conclude that the tactic or agreement is anticompetitive and a violation of the Sherman Act. Causation is not overlooked. No company uses such tactics or agreements without expecting to insulate itself from competition and from the suppression of competition unrelated to efficiency, so it is proper to infer a harm to consumers.

### The American Airlines Case

The government's monopolization case against American Airlines presents something of a puzzle. It is not clear why the Antitrust Agency brought the case, since it has been unable to specify a remedy that is not itself anticompetitive. In fact the remedy requested condemns the government's theory of liability.

The agency contended that American monopolized or attempted to monopolize routes between the Dallas–Fort Worth Airport, the airline's hub, and four cities, the so-called core routes, and did so through predatory pricing or the predatory addition of capacity. The Antitrust Agency also alleged that American monopolized twenty-seven other routes through the reputation it had earned for predatory pricing on the core routes.[20]

The case is best understood as involving the defense of American's hub at Dallas–Fort Worth. Since deregulation, much of the airline industry has moved from offering point-to-point routes to hub-and-spoke routes, a pat-

---

20. Aside from the fact that it depends entirely on a finding of predation on the core routes, this theory of predation by reputation should be dismissed out of hand. It depends on the state of mind of executives whose airlines never attempted entry on a route. No doubt many such executives would testify that they were too frightened to compete, but there would be no way to test the truth of that testimony, and the odds are high that it would be given merely to make American less likely to compete vigorously. Trial by polygraph is hardly a reliable way to resolve antitrust issues.

tern that has enormously increased the efficiency of the carriers. Before deregulation, airlines were certified for trips between specified cities, and city-to-city routes without adequate traffic often went unserved. The hub-and-spoke system changed that. Passengers leaving a small city for many different destinations could be gathered on one plane, transported to a hub, then sent on to their various destinations with passengers who came in from other cities but had the same destination. More routes could be served with more flights.

The efficiency of a hub is thus based on the ability of a hub carrier to serve many more city-pairs and passengers with relatively small increases in costs than it could in a simple point-to-point system. To use an example offered by American, a carrier with two aircraft could serve two routes, San Jose to Nashville and San Diego to Tampa. By employing four ground crews and flying two aircraft 4,033 miles each way, the carrier could compete for the 145 passengers a day each way that fly on those two routes.

When this same carrier serves the same four cities but through Dallas–Fort Worth, the increases in service are dramatic. By connecting passengers at a hub, the carrier serves San Jose–Tampa and San Diego–Nashville as before, but it adds DFW–San Jose, DFW–Tampa, DFW–Nashville, and DFW–San Diego. The passenger boarding at San Jose can still fly to Nashville but is able also to fly to Dallas–Fort Worth, San Diego, and Tampa. The same advantage is given the other three cities of the original four and, in addition, round trips between each of those cities and Dallas–Fort Worth become available for the first time. With the same aircraft, but by hiring two more ground crews and flying a few more miles, the carrier can serve four times as many city pairs and compete for more than ten times as many passengers as before. The efficiencies multiply as the number of spokes at the hub increases and allows hub·carriers to offer many more departures throughout the day from any given city to the hub.

Although the government framed its case as involving attempts by American to preserve supracompetitive returns on the four spoke routes, it is obvious that American would defend its position on those routes even though it made only a competitive rate of return on each. The spoke routes are essential to the efficiency of the hub. The government's attempt to lessen American's ability to preserve its market share on the spokes is thus an attack on the hub system and the efficiencies it creates.

Of the top nine airlines in the country, eight operate hubs. It is not necessary that each operate out of the same hubs because it is possible to fly to and from the same cities through hubs located in different places. This means that there is competition among different airlines' hubs, as well as between airlines at each hub. Thus, the Dallas–Fort Worth hub competes with TWA's hub at St. Louis, Continental's at Houston, America West's at Phoenix, and Southwest's at Love Field near Dallas, plus hubs at Denver and Salt Lake City. Nor is it easy even for a major airline to establish a successful hub. In recent years, for example, American has attempted to establish hubs at San Jose, Nashville, and Raleigh. Each attempt failed. American now has only two hubs, Dallas–Fort Worth and Chicago's O'Hare. It shares DFW as a hub with Delta and O'Hare with United. There is, of course, competition from other airlines that fly in and out of those cities.

Consumers traveling to and from a hub city benefit from nonstop service that is often extraordinarily frequent, far beyond what traffic to and from the hub city alone could support. For example, from Dallas–Fort Worth, American offers eighteen flights a day to New York's LaGuardia Airport and twelve to Washington's Reagan National Airport. Even if American were to carry all local (point-to-point) traffic on these routes, the traffic would support fewer than seven flights to LaGuardia and just five to Washington (assuming the airline were to operate 139-passenger MD-80s at 67 percent load factors).

The efficiencies of hubs also benefit consumers by creating more frequent connecting service between cities that have only a few passengers a day. For example, passengers wishing to travel from Wichita, Kansas, to College Station, Texas, have five American flights a day to choose from, even though an analysis of American's passenger traffic records indicates that on average fewer than two passengers a day travel between Wichita and College Station. Along the same lines, American today offers seven daily nonstop flights between Dallas–Fort Worth and Wichita and publishes connecting service from Wichita to more than eighty cities across the country and around the world. No point-to-point carrier could possibly provide this comprehensive service to a city of Wichita's size.

The specific acts of predation alleged on the four core routes were these. When a so-called low-cost carrier began service on one of the four routes and charged lower fares, American lowered its fares to the same level and increased its capacity on that route to serve the greater demand created by the lower fares. The government, perhaps realizing that meeting the lower fares looked like the competition the Sherman Act is supposed to encourage, shifted from challenging pricing to claiming that American's addition of capacity was a predatory tactic.

The Supreme Court has ruled that to avoid mistakenly characterizing legitimate price competition as predatory, and thereby suppressing competition, two elements must be established before a section 2 violation may be found. First, the alleged predator's prices must be below an appropriate measure of cost. Second, the accused company must have a dangerous probability of recouping its investment in below-cost prices. Although the Supreme Court has never clarified the point, the lower courts are nearly unanimous that the appropriate measure of cost is average variable cost.

The shift from a claim of low pricing to one of increased productivity (the capacity increases) is particularly difficult because price and output are inextricably intertwined. To reduce prices and still serve all the demand (which the district court said doubled or tripled with the reduced fares), the capacity provided by additional flights on a route had to be increased. The alternative would be to lower prices but refuse to serve all the customer demand. That would lead either to rationing and angry customers or to a surrender of all of the additional business to the new entrant.

American's motion for summary judgment pointed out that on each core route its revenues were always above the average variable cost. American also raised the defense of meeting competition because it met, but never undercut, a new entrant's prices. The government argued that meeting competition is a Robinson-Patman Act defense that is not applicable to the Sherman Act. That is peculiar on its face because Robinson-Patman is by far the more stringent statute, and it seems odd the act should grant a freedom to compete that the Sherman Act denies. That would raise the interesting if preposterous possibility that when a large company lowers its price to meet a competitor's price, it has an absolute defense under the Robinson-Patman Act but violates the Sherman Act.

The argument for an absolute defense of meeting competition in an action under section 2 of the Sherman Act is grounded in the nature of the act and in considerations that rise to the constitutional level. Consider the standards available to a court both in determining liability and framing a remedy. There are only two possible fare levels that have any objective basis and do not, therefore, thrust the court into a completely legislative and regulatory role. One is the fare that American charged before the entry of a new competitor. The other is the fare that the new entrant sets and American meets. For the government to win, it would have to assert that American may not alter either its fares or capacity in any respect once entry takes place.

The court cannot, consistently with antitrust principles, hold that American must maintain its previous fare and suffer the loss of its business either instantly or gradually as the entrant adds capacity. That would decrease efficiency, and thus consumer welfare, for the sole purpose of protecting a less efficient competitor. But if the alternative of meeting the lower fare of the entrant is ruled out as an absolute defense, both the court and American would be left completely at sea. The lawful American fare must then be somewhere between American's original fare and the entrant's fare.

There are two difficulties with this conclusion, each fatal to a case. First, the court would have to legislate regulatory standards, a task wholly incompatible with the philosophy of antitrust policy. If, for example, American's original fare was $100 between DFW and city A and the new entrant charged $50, the rejection of the meeting-competition defense would require the court to decide whether American should have charged $60 or $70 or some other fare in between its preentry fare and the entrant's fare. Because the decision could only be made subjectively, the court having no objective criteria on which to rely, American could not know in advance what fare to charge.

The situation would be made equally impossible if the court accepted the government's argument that any defense of meeting competition could not simply match fares but must also take into account any superiority of American's service to that of the new entrant. The court would have to adjust American's allowable fare decrease by considering whether American used jets and the entrant did not, the comparative convenience of flight times, nonstop versus one-stop or connecting flights, the respective values of frequent flyer plans, the value of ticket restrictions, records of on-time arrivals, quality of meals served, seating capacities offered, advertising expenditures, consumer perceptions of the two airlines, and so on. The substance of each decree would have to vary with the competitive strength of the entrant, whether it was Delta, Southwest, or an airline similar to Bob Newhart's invention, which, if memory serves, was Mrs. Ferguson's Storm Door and Airline Company. Only after assessing, or guessing at, the dollar value of these factors on each route could the court arrive at the amount American was required to charge above the fare the entrant charged.

That would by no means be the end of the matter. All other major airlines would be subject to the same requirements. To avoid inconsistencies, these cases would have to be brought into the same district court. As conditions changed, which they do constantly in this industry, the allowable fares and capacities on each route would have to be continually adjusted for each major airline. The government's argument, if accepted, would produce a regulatory nightmare—all in the name of a statute that is based on the idea of free competitive actions and responses.

It is probably for this reason that courts applying the Robinson-Patman Act have refused to compare products to adjust the price required to qualify for the meeting-competition defense. It is doubtful, moreover, that any of those cases presented as many variables as does the airline industry. The court would be converted into a rate-making agency, a sort of Interstate Commerce Commission for the airline industry. That would be doubly perverse given Congress's decision to deregulate the airline industry. The government's proposal to re-regulate airlines through antitrust litigation, in addition to the proposal's other defects, would thus defy Congress's policy decision. And any court that took on regulation of the minutiae of the air travel industry would have no room left on its docket for other cases. The government's proposed remedy is that for two years American could not add capacity on any route where a new entrant appears. The entrant would be given a major share of the market by judicial decree, no matter what passengers wanted. That would take antitrust law back to the discredited era when efficiency and consumer welfare were sacrificed for the welfare of competitors.

Constitutional problems of due process and the political question doctrine would obviously arise. Because neither American nor any other major airline would receive fair warning and thus could only guess in advance what a court might decide, perhaps years later, were allowable fare decreases and capacity increases, the airlines would be vulnerable to government civil or criminal prosecution and to triple damage awards in private suits. To provide fair warning, a court would have to enter incredibly detailed decrees in advance of any incumbent's response to new entry. The incumbent, however, could not afford to wait years or even months before it could compete to the extent the court might ultimately allow. Some provision would have to be made for the interim period between entry and judicial guidance.

But none of this would solve the political question. Antitrust lawyers may think it odd to raise that doctrine in an antitrust case, but its formulation in *Baker* v. *Carr* fits the situation exactly.[21] Justice William Brennan, writing for a Supreme Court majority, stated that the doctrine flows from

---

21. *Baker* v. *Carr*, 369 U.S. 186, 217 (1962).

the separation of powers. Among the criteria he specified for application of the doctrine were "a lack of judicially discoverable and manageable standards for resolving [the issue]; or the impossibility of deciding without an initial policy determination of a kind clearly for nonjudicial discretion." Antitrust courts have applied those tests in refusing to accept the reasonable-price defense for price fixing, and in a series of cases made these criteria the standards for upholding or denying the constitutionality of statutes regulating competition.[22] *United States* v. *Cohen Grocery Co.* employed the Fifth and Sixth Amendments to invalidate section 4 of the Lever Act, a federal criminal statute that provided "it is hereby made unlawful for any person willfully . . . to make any unjust or unreasonable rate or charge in handling or dealing in or with any necessaries; to conspire, combine, agree, or arrange with any other person . . . to exact excessive prices for any necessaries."[23] Chief Justice Edward White, the author of the 1911 *Standard Oil* and *American Tobacco* decisions that framed the modern rule of reason,[24] wrote for the Court in *Cohen Grocery.*

> Observe that the section forbids no specific or definite act. It confines the subject-matter of the investigation which it authorizes to no element essentially inhering in the transaction as to which it provides. It leaves open, therefore, the widest conceivable inquiry, the scope of which no one can foreshadow or adequately guard against. In fact, we see no reason to doubt the soundness of the observation of the court below, in its opinion, to the effect that, to attempt to enforce the section would be the exact equivalent of an effort to carry out a statute which in terms merely penalized and punished all acts detrimental to the public interest when unjust and unreasonable in the estimation of the court and jury.

These cases were typically decided under the due process clauses as void because of vagueness and failure to provide fair warning. The distinction between due process and the political-question doctrine thus appears to be that due process demands fairness for the person subject to the law while the doctrine demands, in the name of the separation of powers, that courts withhold judgment when there are no judicially discoverable and manageable standards or when an initial policy determination of a kind

---

22. These matters are discussed more fully in Bork (1993, pp. 72–80).

23. *United States* v. *Cohen Grocery Co.*, 255 U.S. 81, 89 (1921).

24. *United States* v. *Standard Oil* 221 U.S. 1 (1911); *United States* v. *American Tobacco Co.* 221 U.S. 106 (1911).

clearly for nonjudicial discretion would be required. Although one concept protects the person to whom the law would be applied and the other protects the constitutional division of functions, they come together in defeating attempted government prosecutions of cases like that against American Airlines.

This examination of the high-stakes antitrust cases brought during the Clinton administration suggests that two of them were well founded in law and economics and therefore that similar cases are likely to be brought in the future. The two also suggest that network effects are forms of efficiency and not to be attacked under the antitrust laws as illegitimate barriers to competition. Finally, they suggest that networks do not lead to monopoly where competitors, network or independent, are in the field (as in *American Airlines*) or when the possessors of the network think they must resort to predation or conspiracy to maintain their monopolistic positions (as in *Microsoft* and *Visa/Mastercard*).

## Reference

Bork, Robert. 1993. *The Antitrust Paradox,* rev. ed. with a new introduction and epilogue. Free Press.

HOWARD H. CHANG
DAVID S. EVANS
RICHARD SCHMALENSEE

4

# *Has the Consumer Harm Standard Lost Its Teeth?*

T here appears to be universal agreement that
antitrust policy should "protect competition, not
competitors" and that consumer welfare is the fundamental standard for
evaluating the effects of competition.[1] There is considerable debate, however, about how to put those principles into practice when evaluating rule-

The authors thank Bryan Martin-Keating and Nese Nasif for research assistance and Visa for financial support. The authors have consulted for Microsoft and Visa—two of the defendants in cases discussed in this article. Robert Bork's chapter in this volume, "High-States Antitrust: The Last Hurrah?"
takes direct aim at a number of points we make here. We have responded to some of his comments in
our footnotes.

1. *Brown Shoe Co.* v. *United States*, 370 U.S. 294, 320 (1962): "the legislative history illuminates con-
gressional concern with the protection of competition, not competitors." *Reiter* v. *Sonotone Corp.*, 442
U.S. 330, 343 (1979): "Congress designed the Sherman Act as a 'consumer welfare prescription.'" Bork
(1978): "The only legitimate goal of American antitrust law is the maximization of consumer welfare."
Litan and Shapiro (2002): "For at least 20 years a broad, bipartisan consensus has prevailed regarding
the goal of U.S. antitrust policy: to foster competitive markets and to control monopoly power, not to
protect smaller firms from tough competition by larger corporations. The interests of consumers in
lower prices and improved products are paramount." Social welfare, which would include producer surplus in addition to consumer surplus, and, perhaps equivalently, efficiency are also sometimes mentioned as goals for antitrust policy. Carlton and Perloff (2000); Bork (1978, pp. 91, 104–106, 409–10,
416, 427–29); Posner (2001). It is unclear whether the courts generally consider effects on producer
surplus an important factor. In addition, the inquiry in merger cases as to whether cost savings are
passed on to consumers instead of being retained by the merged firm reflects a clear preference for consumer gains over producer gains. Despite the consensus about protecting competition and consumers,

of-reason antitrust claims under the Sherman Act. Some commentators focus on the need to show that substantial consumer harm in the form of significantly higher prices or lower output either has occurred or plausibly could occur before condemning a practice as anticompetitive.[2] Other commentators contend that sufficient consumer harm to establish a violation can be inferred indirectly from harm to competition or what they characterize as "harm to the competitive process." Under some versions of this second standard the question of substantiality does not arise; it is only necessary to show some harm to actual or nascent competitors.[3] The crux of the debate is over the relative frequency and cost of false convictions versus false acquittals and the extent to which the courts can confidently predict the effects of challenged practices on consumer welfare given the evidence, including economic theory and empirical studies, available to them.

The Clinton administration invited the courts to rely on a relatively weak consumer harm standard for assessing liability in antitrust cases brought against Intel, Microsoft, and Visa and MasterCard.[4] The government adopted the view that it was enough to show that the challenged practices had harmed the competitive process—we argue it did not even make that showing. The government also believed that direct evidence that the challenged practices, on balance, raised prices, lowered output, or reduced quality and thereby reduced consumer welfare was not needed. In the two cases that went to trial and for which there is a complete record—*United States* v. *Microsoft* and *United States* v. *Visa*—the district court accepted this view.[5] And in the one case that has gone to an appeals court—*Microsoft*—the District of Columbia Circuit Court affirmed liability without reaching findings that the anticompetitive actions resulted

---

the courts are far from consistent in applying this standard. See Fox (2002): "A number of contemporary cases on exclusionary practices tend to be noncommittal if not obfuscatory in their usage of 'anticompetitive.' Yet others openly aver that the antitrust laws protect competition, not efficiency, and that the absence of consumer harm is no obstacle to a judgment for the plaintiff."

2. See Evans (2001); Joffe (2001). We regard "significant" and "substantial" as synonyms and use them interchangeably.

3. Salop and Romaine (1999); Houck (2001).

4. During the Clinton years, antitrust enforcers displayed an increased "confidence that they could correct market failures in the realm of innovation." Litan and Shapiro (2000, p. 436). We refer to the Clinton administration's antitrust enforcers as the "government." The states and the District of Columbia were also plaintiffs in the Microsoft litigation. When necessary, we distinguish actions taken by the federal and state antitrust enforcers.

5. *United States* v. *Microsoft*, 253 F.3d 34 (2001); *United States* v. *Visa U.S.A. et al.*, 163 F. Supp. 2d 322 (2001).

in substantial harm to consumers.[6] It specifically found that the district court's findings do not demonstrate that there was a causal relationship between those actions and any significant changes in the competitive process that could lead to substantial harm and directed the lower court to address causation as part of the examination of remedies.[7] The court itself described the standard it employed as "edentulous"—toothless.[8] We argue in general and in the context of these two cases that this weaker standard represents economically unsound policy.

This chapter develops and explores two important differences between those who insist on direct proof of harm to consumers and those who are willing to infer consumer harm from harm to competitors.[9] First, and arguably technically, what preconditions must hold for it to be valid to infer injury to consumers indirectly from injury to one or more competitors? In neither *Microsoft* nor *Visa* did the courts require antitrust enforcers to establish critical preconditions. The second difference is whether a showing of *substantial* harm to consumers should be required for liability. We argue here that such a requirement is necessary for sound policy. A

6. The court did assert that Microsoft's actions had "significant" and "substantial" effects, but it did so without support in its opinion or the trial record. More critically, the court said that it could not infer that Microsoft's actions had or were likely to have a significant effect on maintaining its monopoly. See Fox (2002, p. 390): "It was perhaps a misnomer for the court to say, at numerous points, 'this conduct had a substantial effect in protecting Microsoft's market power'—for, finally, we are told that the court did not know, and that it is fine to be agnostic about this unproved proposition."

7. *United States* v. *Microsoft*, 253 F.3d 34, 106–07 (2001). See also Memorandum Opinion, *State of New York, et al.* v. *Microsoft*, Civil Action No. 98-1233 (CKK) Nov. 1, 2002, 21: "In addition, the appellate court reiterated its concern over the quantum of proof provided to support a causal connection between the exclusionary conduct and Microsoft's persistence in the dominant market position."

8. *United States* v. *Microsoft*, 253 F.3d 34, 79 (2001).

9. Bork believes that we have offered a false choice and that the real choice is "between those who insist on direct proof of consumer harm and those who think that consumer harm can be inferred from certain forms of exclusionary market behavior that cannot be shown to create or maintain efficiency" (p. 60). He also criticizes us for failing to consider the efficiencies stage. Our focus in this chapter is on the consumer harm stage of the analysis, which, as we have argued elsewhere, should precede the efficiencies stage because we have well established methods for analyzing competitive effects, whereas the evaluation of efficiencies is more difficult. Chang and others (1998, pp. 276–78). In his previous writings, Bork has noted he believes the difficulty of showing cost efficiencies in the merger context is so great as to be unworkable. Bork (1978, pp. 123–29). It is likely that demonstrating efficiencies from organizational rules, such as those at issue in *Visa*, is likely even more difficult.

Where we differ from Bork is regarding whether one needs to do any analysis of consumer harm before getting to the second (efficiencies) stage or whether one can just do a "quick look." Except for practices that are per se illegal or close—practices for which past analysis or case law is enough to predict effects reliably—analysis is necessary to show that the practice is indeed "exclusionary" or "restric-

finding of liability generally implies the imposition of structural or behavioral relief that, by design, reduces the competitive effectiveness of the defendant (generally a leading firm and, in section 2 cases, the market leader). It thus commonly imposes nontrivial costs on both that firm and, potentially, consumers. Without the likelihood of substantial offsetting benefits from strengthening competition from other sources, such relief, even if it does not go beyond an order to cease some facially suspect practices that pass a minimal consumer harm standard, is more likely than not to harm consumers on balance.

The remainder of this chapter discusses the general issues in more detail. It then uses an error-cost framework to explain why it is economically important to require plaintiffs to show (directly or indirectly) that a challenged practice actually imposes or is highly likely to impose significant consumer harm. Next, the *Microsoft* and *Visa* cases are used to illustrate how the Clinton Antitrust Division's failure to undertake analyses that could have ascertained whether there was significant harm to competitors and competition led the courts to mistake protecting competitor profits for protecting consumer welfare. A final section summarizes our major conclusions and considers whether the weak consumer harm standard successfully employed by the Clinton Administration in the *Microsoft* and *Visa* cases will establish an enduring legacy of activist antitrust. We conclude that the Clinton standard is inconsistent with the thrust of antitrust jurisprudence over the last twenty years so that it will become a legacy only if the Supreme Court makes a sharp turn.

## The Consumer Harm Standard

Although the Supreme Court has not delineated a particular standard for assessing consumer harm in antitrust cases, it has touched on the principles for determining harm. The most detailed treatment involves determining the circumstances under which pricing low is anticompetitive. The Court has addressed this matter in two leading predatory pricing cases,

---

tive" in economic, as opposed to linguistic, terms. Bork appears to believe that being facially suspect should generally be enough to lose a rule-of-reason section 2 case when the defendants are unable to demonstrate efficiencies to the court's satisfaction. We disagree and would require a real showing of consumer harm.

*Matsushita* v. *Zenith* and *Brooke Group* v. *Brown & Williamson.* Together these decisions have resulted in what is known as the *Brooke Group* test, which emphasizes the need to show harm to consumers rather than harm to competitors.

### The Brooke Group Test

There are two main elements to the *Brooke Group* test, which establishes the standard for a showing of predation (where the defendant is accused of setting low prices to drive competitors out of business). First, a plaintiff alleging predation must show that the defendant's prices were "below an appropriate measure of . . . costs."[10] Thus pricing must be below cost to support a claim of predation, even though in theory there can be predatory prices that are above cost.[11] Second, the plaintiff must show that the defendant had "a reasonable prospect, or, under §2 of the Sherman Act, a dangerous probability, of recouping its investment in below-cost prices."[12] That is, finding that prices were low enough to inconvenience a competitor is not enough. Logically, for recoupment to be reasonably likely, low prices must eliminate substantial competition in a way that persists even after a postpredation price increase.

The *Brooke Group* test provides what we would consider to be a sound standard for assessing whether low prices are predatory. In *Brooke Group* and *Matsushita* the Court gave two reasons that fit into an error-cost framework.[13] First, "predatory pricing schemes are rarely tried, and even more rarely successful," whereas "cutting prices in order to increase business often is the very essence of competition." Because the Court believed predation to be uncommon, it was more concerned with judicial mistakes that would wrongly condemn procompetitive price cutting. Second, the Court noted that "mistaken inferences [in predation cases] are especially costly, because they chill the very conduct [vigorous price competition] the antitrust laws are designed to protect."[14] That is, the cost of mistakenly condemning procompetitive price cutting is particularly high. These two reasons suggest that the courts should be most concerned about lowering

10. *Brooke Group Ltd.* v. *Brown & Williamson Tobacco Corp.*, 509 U.S. 209, 222 (1993).

11. Denger and Herfort (1994, p. 541).

12. *Brooke Group* v. *Brown & Williamson*, 222.

13. Both decisions cite Easterbrook (1984), which discusses an error-cost approach to antitrust analysis. See *Matsushita* v. *Zenith*, 475 U.S. 574, 591 (1986); *Brooke Group* v. *Brown & Williamson*, 233.

14. *Matsushita* v. *Zenith*, 589, 594 , quoted in *Brooke Group* v. *Brown & Williamson*, 226.

the error cost from false convictions (versus false acquittals) in predation cases. This is what the Court did in *Matsushita* and *Brooke Group* when it required evidence of below-cost pricing as well as evidence on likely reduction in competition and likely recoupment of losses suffered during the alleged predatory period.[15] It is worth noting that the second of these reasons—concern for the chilling effect on procompetitive behavior—applies to a variety of antitrust claims that involve, in essence, charges of competing too hard.

In other contexts the Supreme Court has also rebuffed attempts to infer consumer harm from theoretical musings. Its reasoning in the *California Dental* decision is instructive.[16] The Federal Trade Commission (FTC) had argued that certain advertising restrictions, including restrictions affecting price advertising, adopted by a dentists' association in California were anticompetitive. The FTC was sure enough of its case that it did not have an economist testify as to whether consumers had been harmed. In some literal sense, one could argue that the advertising restriction restrained competition, that competitors faced restrictions on the type of advertising they could employ. But in the absence of empirical evidence, that literal argument fails to show that consumers were actually harmed.

The Ninth Circuit Court of Appeals endorsed the FTC's argument. The Supreme Court, however, rejected the characterization of the advertising restrictions as naked restrictions on price and insisted on actual evidence, especially empirical evidence, of consumer harm:

> But these observations brush over the professional context and describe no anticompetitive effects. Assuming that the record in fact supports the conclusion that the CDA [California Dental Association] disclosure rules essentially bar advertisement of across-the-board discounts, it does not obviously follow that such a ban would have a net anticompetitive effect here. Whether advertisements that announced discounts for, say, first-time customers, would be less effective at conveying information relevant to competition if they listed the original and discounted prices for checkups, X-rays, and fillings, than they would be if they simply specified a percentage discount across the board, *seems to us a question susceptible to empirical but not a priori analysis.*

---

15. *Matsushita* v. *Zenith*, 475 U.S. 574, 588 (1986). The recoupment standard was more explicitly developed in *Brooke Group Ltd.* v. *Brown & Williamson Tobacco Corp.*, 509 U.S. 209, 224 (1993).

16. *California Dental Association* v. *FTC*, 526 U.S. 756 (1999). See also *NYNEX Corp.* v. *Discon, Inc.*, 525 U.S. 128, 135 (1998) ("the plaintiff here must allege and prove harm, not just to a single competitor, but to the competitive process, i.e., to competition itself.").

[Justice Stephen Breyer] thinks that the Commission and the Court of Appeals "adequately answered that question," ibid., *but the absence of any empirical evidence on this point indicates that the question was not answered,* merely avoided by implicit burden-shifting of the kind accepted by Justice Breyer. The point is that before a theoretical claim of anticompetitive effects can justify shifting to a defendant the burden to show empirical evidence of procompetitive effects, as quick-look analysis in effect requires, there must be some indication that the court making the decision has properly identified the theoretical basis for the anticompetitive effects and considered whether the effects actually are anticompetitive. Where, as here, the circumstances of the restriction are somewhat complex, *assumption alone will not do.*[17]

On remand, the Ninth Circuit Court looked at the facts in the record and ruled against the FTC.[18] The Supreme Court has not, however, addressed the proper standard for assessing consumer harm generally in rule-of-reason cases (where the practice challenged is not found to be illegal per se) or for specific practices other than predatory pricing that often come under the rule-of-reason rubric. Nevertheless, the error-cost framework implicit in *Brooke Group* can be extended to these other practices. First, however, it is useful to describe the approach toward consumer harm advocated by the Clinton antitrust enforcers.

### Clinton Administration Approach

A canonical view of the Clinton approach, based on a review of *Microsoft, Visa,* and *Intel* goes roughly as follows.[19] First, the government pre-

17. *California Dental Association* v. *FTC,* 526 U.S. 756, 775 (1999) (emphasis added).

18. We are not suggesting—nor do we believe the court was—that the practices engaged in by the California Dental Association are not suspect. The point is that the plaintiff should bear the burden of showing that practices such as these are suspect. If they are clearly anticompetitive as Justice Breyer asserted, the plaintiff should have an easy time making such a showing.

19. Because *Intel* was settled before trial, the publicly available record does not permit us to discuss the case in as much detail as we do below for *Microsoft* and *Visa,* but the antitrust philosophy of the enforcement agencies during the Clinton administration can also be seen in *Intel.* In response to separate patent infringement suits from three of its customers, Intel withheld from those customers the right to use certain intellectual property. The Federal Trade Commission argued that Intel's behavior was a means of "coercing" licenses to their rival microprocessor technology, thereby maintaining and strengthening Intel's monopoly in the general-purpose microprocessor market. The available evidence provides little support for the existence of significant consumer harm. Of the three companies at issue, only one was even a competitor in the relevant market for general-purpose microprocessors, and that company's executives testified that its microprocessor research and development efforts were not harmed as a result of Intel's conduct: Intel Corporation's Trial Brief, Public Version, FTC Docket

sented evidence to demonstrate that competitors were harmed. Second, it presented evidence to demonstrate that those harmed were important competitors (either actual or potential) in concentrated markets, so that harm to them constituted harm to competition or to the competitive process. The government believed this was sufficient for a finding of liability because harm to consumers could be inferred from harm to competition or to the competitive process.[20]

It is important to distinguish analytically between three terms that are often used in this context: *harm to competitors, harm to competition or to the competitive process,* and *harm to consumers.*[21] There is little debate about what harm to competitors and harm to consumers mean. Harm to competitors occurs when a competitor is disadvantaged—for example, faces higher costs or lower demand as a result of the challenged action. Harm to consumers occurs when, for example, prices are higher or industry output lower as a result of the challenged action. There is, however, considerable debate about what constitutes harm to competition.

If harm to competition were synonymous with harm to consumers, which is the convention adopted by some commentators and is our preferred definition, there would be no dispute that significant harm to competition would be a sufficient basis for antitrust liability. During the Clinton

---

No. 9218 (Feb. 25, 1999), 12–13. The commission also failed to produce evidence of any likely significant harm to Intel customers' incentives to innovate or to the incentives of any other firms in the microprocessor industry. Although the FTC settled its case against Intel with a consent decree, the Court of Appeals for the Federal Circuit dismissed similar antitrust claims in a private lawsuit against Intel, saying, "Although Intergraph stresses the adverse effect on its business of Intel's proposed withdrawal of these special benefits, the record evidence contains no analysis of the effect of such action on competition among manufacturers of graphics subsystems or high-end workstations." *Intergraph Corp.* v. *Intel Corp.*, 195 F.3d 1346, 1355 (1999).

20. Bork says that this description is overly "simplified." He contends, with approval, that "the government was required to show behavior of the sort that was likely to harm competitors illegitimately and thus cause harm to the competitive process" (p. 61). Under his formulation "illegitimate" competitor harm equates with consumer harm. This requires no economic analysis, no showing of injury to anyone—it is trial by labeling. As the Chicago School of Economics made clear long ago, and as experience in complex cases like *Microsoft* and *Visa* illustrates, debates about labels are a poor substitute indeed for careful analysis of actual economic effects, particularly in complex organizations or rapidly changing markets. Note also that Bork explicitly equates harm to competitors (as long as it fits in an "illegitimate" category) with harm to the competitive process. This is either sloppy economics or a clear and surprising departure from basic antitrust principles.

21. To add to the confusion about terminology, some commentators use harm to competition interchangeably with harm to consumers. As we discuss, the Clinton approach sometimes refers to harm to competition as harm to the competitive process and regards both as something short of harm to consumers.

administration, however, antitrust enforcers often seemed to emphasize that plaintiffs did not have to demonstrate consumer harm, thus implying a difference between these two concepts.

For example, the government's main economic witness in *Microsoft* stated: "The presumption of antitrust policy is that competition itself brings consumer benefits, and the lessening of competition brings consumer harm. Hence, *plaintiffs are required to show an injury to competition rather than immediate harm to consumers.*"[22]

Similarly, the lead trial counsel to the state plaintiffs in *Microsoft* has written that there is "*no requirement of proof of actual harm to consumers— beyond that of injury to competition. . . .* Proof of actual consumer harm is not required because it is inferred from injury to competition."[23]

And in *Visa* the government argued, "To show consumer harm, it is not necessary to prove precisely what choices consumers would have made, precisely how individual firms would have tried to respond to consumers, or whether they would have won or lost the competitive battle; *it is sufficient to prove that the challenged restraint had a significant impact on the process by which competitive decisions were made.*"[24]

From these statements, it is evident that the Clinton Justice Department's standard of harm to competition was intended to be distinct from, and less rigorous than, a showing of harm to consumers.

To the extent that the Clinton standard relies on competitor harm, by itself, as a proxy for consumer harm, it is simply wrong as a matter of economics. Competitor harm must be insufficient for antitrust liability because the competitive process, by its very nature, consists of companies trying to gain competitive advantages over other companies. Merely because a firm is disadvantaged does not mean its contribution to market competition is substantially reduced: the disadvantage may be minor, or affect only fixed costs, or the firm may not be an important actual or potential competitor in the first place. And even a substantial reduction in the effectiveness of a few participants in a competitive market may not harm consumers at all if other participants or potential market entrants have the ability and incentive to take up the slack.

We believe there is no meaningful concept of harm to competition in antitrust that does not imply harm to consumers. If there has been signif-

---

22. Evans and others (2000, p. 88, emphasis added).

23. Houck (2001, p. 596, emphasis added).

24. Plaintiffs' Post-Trial Proposed Conclusions of Law, *United States* v. *Visa U.S.A.*, 98 CIV. 7076, Sept. 22, 2000, para. 10 (emphasis added).

icant harm to important competitors in a way that truly matters for competition, it should be straightforward to take the next step and show that harm to consumers is likely. Evidence of likely consumer harm—substantial harmful effects on prices, output, or quality—should be required for antitrust liability in rule-of-reason Sherman Act cases. If it is difficult to show that consumers were harmed or likely will be harmed, that should be a clear signal that any harm to competitors that was found may not have had any significant impact on competition.

In many cases, it will be feasible at reasonable cost to assess consumer harm directly through analyzing effects on price, quantity, or quality. In such cases, plaintiffs should be obliged to present this sort of direct analysis. In other cases, however, direct analysis will be impossible or impractical. For example, if the allegation is that a company has been driven out of business by predation or if a nascent competitor has been prevented from developing into an actual competitor by exclusionary practices, the resulting consumer harm would not appear until later. In such cases a direct analysis of actual consumer harm is not possible. Even when consumer harm is not prospective, it may be practical only to assess the harm indirectly by analysis of impacts on competition. Nevertheless, following *Brooke Group*, competitor harm alone should not be sufficient to establish liability, since it is not sufficient to establish consumer harm. It is analytically correct to infer consumer injury from injury to competitors only if (1) the injury is severe enough to have a significant impact on the competitors' effectiveness; (2) the competitors affected are important enough so that their effectiveness matters to consumers in the short run; and (3) the short-run injury to competition cannot be easily overcome by the market entry or expansion of other firms.[25]

---

25. Bork believes that we have argued "that consumer harm must be proved through direct evidence rather than, as the government and the courts thought, by inference from a showing of the intentional infliction of harm upon competitors without any reason grounded in greater efficiency and consumer welfare" (p. 61). The discussion in the text should make it clear that we believe it can be appropriate to infer consumer harm from competitor harm with the additional analytical steps described, but that the inference cannot be assumed from competitor harm alone. The standard he endorses is that an "intent" to harm competitors is sufficient to make the inference of consumer harm unless the defendant can articulate a "reason grounded in greater efficiency and consumer welfare." He appears to believe that the steps we have outlined are superfluous—that is, that injury to competitors would still be sufficient for antitrust liability even when that injury is not severe enough to significantly limit their effectiveness or where the competitors are unimportant to competition in the relevant market. Bork's approach is particularly problematic when one recognizes the difficulty of distinguishing aggressive competition (which may be designed to inflict injury on competitors but which benefits consumers) from anticompetitive behavior.

In the context of predation, the Supreme Court has explicitly recognized that harm to competitors is insufficient to establish liability. A showing that a competitor has been driven out of business, which would certainly constitute substantial harm to the competitor and to its effectiveness, is not enough. The plaintiff must show that pricing was below cost and that the alleged predator had a "dangerous probability" of recouping its losses from predation. For this to be possible, conditions (2) and (3) must hold. Without these additional requirements the courts would be unable to distinguish instances of harm to competitors that are part of the normal competitive process from instances of competitor harm that may lead to substantial harm to consumers.

In regard to the exclusion of nascent competitors, the appeals court decision in *Microsoft* articulates the analytically correct test—whether "the exclusion of nascent threats is the type of conduct that is reasonably capable of contributing significantly to a defendant's continued monopoly power" and "whether [the firms affected] reasonably constituted nascent threats at the time [the defendant] engaged in the anticompetitive conduct at issue."[26] This test is closely related to the three conditions mentioned earlier, with the second modified to require that the affected firms reasonably constitute important nascent competitors.[27]

Not only did the Clinton administration seem to confuse injury to competitors with injury to competition,[28] as evidenced in *Microsoft*, *Visa*, and *Intel*, it failed to demonstrate *substantiality* of harm, either to competitors or to competition. Let us start with harm to competitors. In *Microsoft* and *Visa* the government identified particular practices used by the defendant (generally practices that would be termed aggressive competition if engaged in by smaller entities) and argued that competitors would have been better off absent those practices.[29] And the respective courts agreed. We argue later in detail that the courts in both cases made findings of competitor harm without requiring an attempt to quantify or otherwise demonstrate the substantiality of that harm, even though there were analy-

---

26. *United States* v. *Microsoft*, 253 F.3d 34, 79 (2001).

27. As we argue later, however, the appeals court failed to apply this test correctly to the acts it upheld as anticompetitive in *Microsoft*.

28. As noted above, Bork, much to our surprise, would apparently not describe this as confusion.

29. *United States* v. *Microsoft*, 253 F.3d 34 (2001); *United States* v. *Visa*, 163 F. Supp.2d 322 (2001). See also note 17 for a discussion of *Intel*.

ses that could have been realistically undertaken that would have shown substantial harm if it had existed.[30]

Without evidence that competitors have been harmed substantially enough to reduce their effectiveness in the marketplace, there can be no meaningful attempt to assess whether harm to some competitors translated into harm to competition overall, let alone substantial harm. Even if substantiality of competitor harm had been shown, it would still be necessary to show that the harm led (or was likely to lead) to substantial harm to consumers. As discussed earlier, there are many reasons why consumer harm does not automatically follow from competitor harm, even substantial competitor harm. Since the government was relying on its inference of harm to consumers from harm to competitors, it made no attempt to demonstrate directly that consumers had been (or were likely to be) harmed significantly in the form of higher prices, lower quality or lower output.

The Clinton administration's approach to consumer harm is in stark contrast to the approach laid out by the Supreme Court in the *Brooke Group* test. Even a showing of substantial harm to competitors in a highly concentrated market is not enough under the test. Additional evidence is needed that the harm to competitors comes from anticompetitive rather than procompetitive behavior and is likely to lead to the long-term elimination of competition. The government's approach, however, permits inferences of harm to competition from harm to competitors without requiring examination of the conditions that must be satisfied to validate such an inference.

## An Error-Cost Analysis

The discussion that follows uses an error-cost analysis to discuss the standard required for showing significant consumer harm in rule-of-reason Sherman Act cases. A weaker standard of evidence of consumer harm increases the likelihood of "false convictions," condemning procompetitive practices. A stronger standard increases the likelihood of "false acquittals,"

---

30. In *Microsoft*, the appeals court reduced the set of acts found anticompetitive but failed to require a reexamination to determine whether the remaining anticompetitive acts had caused significant harm to Navigator or Java as competitors to Windows.

exonerating anticompetitive practices.[31] The standard used by the Clinton antitrust enforcers strikes that balance in the wrong place: it is too weak and leads to too many false convictions. We advocate a more stringent standard that would require evidence that consumers have been harmed substantially or, in the case of prospective harm, evidence that consumers would likely be harmed substantially. This stronger standard would necessarily reduce false convictions. However, the more stringent standard is one that can realistically be met by plaintiffs in cases where the challenged behavior is in fact anticompetitive, a point that we demonstrate in our analysis of the *Microsoft* and *Visa* cases. Consequently, our standard would result in a minimal increase in false acquittals.

### Basic Framework

The frequency of false convictions and false acquittals depends in part on the burden of proof and other standards of evidence. Civil antitrust cases are decided based on the preponderance of the evidence. That is generally taken to mean that if it is more likely than not that the defendant's actions are anticompetitive, the defendant is convicted (and conversely, if it is more likely than not that the defendant's actions are not anticompetitive, the defendant is acquitted). The frequencies of false convictions and of false acquittals also depend on what must be shown: in this context, how seriously the courts take the requirement that consumer harm is significant. Almost any action taken by a major company is likely to make some consumers unhappy, just as all contracts necessarily restrain trade.[32] As the standards for determining what constitutes significant consumer harm and what evidence is necessary to show its existence become weaker, the likelihood of false convictions increases. In terms of social cost, the problem is not such errors themselves or even the unjustified monetary damage awards to which they give rise. The social costs associated with these awards, which are primarily transfers, are relatively small. Social costs can be significant, however, when a practice that would improve efficiency is barred, a leading firm is forced to compete less effectively, or structural relief directly impairs productive efficiency.

---

31. See generally Posner (1999). "Acquittal" and "conviction" are borrowed from the criminal context for convenience, even though the antitrust litigation discussed in this chapter is civil, not criminal. This is the same terminology used in Beckner and Salop (1999, p. 41); Hylton and Salinger (2001, p. 469).

32. *United States* v. *Addyston Pipe & Steel Co.*, 78 F.712, 721 (1897).

Consider a simple model with the following parameters. The probability that the challenged action is in fact anticompetitive and has thus actually caused consumer harm is $p$. There is no "true" uncertainty regarding whether an action is anticompetitive—it is either anticompetitive or it is not. The court, however, does not know ex ante whether the defendant is innocent or guilty, only that the proportion of anticompetitive actions among the population of actions challenged is $p$.

The probability that a defendant is falsely convicted is $x_c(s)$, where $s$ is the standard required for a showing of consumer harm.[33] That is, for a case where the challenged conduct should be permitted, $x_c(s)$ is the probability that the court makes a mistake and finds the defendant liable. Similarly, the probability of a false acquittal, permitting conduct that is anticompetitive, is $x_a(s)$. The probability of both false acquittals and false convictions depends on $s$. We define a higher $s$ to be associated with a stricter standard. As $s$ becomes more stringent, $x_c(s)$ generally decreases because it is less likely that a defendant is falsely convicted when a greater showing of consumer harm is required. Similarly, as $s$ becomes more stringent, $x_a(s)$ generally increases. Finally, one must also consider the relative costs to society of false convictions ($c_c$) and false acquittals ($c_a$). The cost of a false conviction, $c_c$, is the loss in welfare because firms are prevented from engaging in the practice that has been wrongly prohibited and the impact of any other associated relief that might be imposed. Similarly, the cost of a false acquittal is the loss in welfare from failing to prohibit the conduct that is in fact anticompetitive.

The total cost of judicial errors is the sum of the respective error costs from false convictions and false acquittals. First, consider the error cost resulting from false convictions. The probability (across all cases) that a given case involves a defendant that is falsely convicted is equal to the probability a given defendant is innocent $(1 - p)$ multiplied by the probability that an innocent defendant is wrongly convicted, $x_c(s)$. The cost of a false conviction is $c_c$, so that the expected error cost (per case) from false convictions is $(1 - p)^*x_c(s)^*c_c$. Similarly, the cost of false acquittals is equal to the frequency of false acquittals multiplied by their costs, or $p^*x_a(s)^*c_a$. The

---

33. The standard $s$ could also include other aspects of the process, such as the preponderance standard and allocations of burdens of proof. We focus on the consumer harm standard. In addition, for simplicity, we assume that the probability $p$ that a defendant has behaved anticompetitively does not depend on $s$, which may not be true if the standard of proof affects the cases brought by plaintiffs. Our discussion later, which is qualitative, would still hold.

total expected error cost (per case) is the sum of the costs from these two types of errors or $x_c(s)*(1-p)* c_c + x_a(s)*p* c_a$. The natural objective for policy is to minimize the total expected error cost by choice of the standard, $s$, for finding consumer harm.

### Effect of the Consumer Harm Standard on Error Costs

The socially optimal consumer harm standard depends on beliefs about the relative size of the marginal error costs from false convictions versus those from false acquittals. If the marginal error cost from false convictions (the decreased error cost resulting from a decrease in false convictions from increasing the standard $s$ slightly) is relatively high, society should favor requiring a stricter standard for consumer harm. Conversely, if the marginal error cost from false convictions is relatively low then a looser standard for consumer harm would be appropriate.

Antitrust jurisprudence to some extent implicitly reflects this sort of error-cost analysis. This can be seen in the evidence required by the courts in recent years for predatory pricing. One can also see this reflection in the context of the standard of proof in criminal versus that in civil cases. In criminal cases society has decided that "it is better to acquit ten guilty defendants than convict one innocent one." That is, the social cost of a false conviction greatly outweighs that of a false acquittal. Thus the standard of proof in a criminal case is "beyond a reasonable doubt" rather than the "preponderance of the evidence" standard in civil cases.

In our simple model three factors determine the relative size of marginal error costs from false convictions versus those from false acquittals: marginal change in false convictions versus false acquittals from changing the current consumer harm standard (the size of $dx_c/ds$ versus $dx_a/ds$), the probability $p$ that a given defendant is guilty, and the size of $c_c$ versus that of $c_a$. We now explain why consideration of these factors indicates that the standard for consumer harm advocated by the Clinton antitrust enforcers and accepted in whole or in part by some courts is too low.

ERROR PROBABILITIES: $dx_c/ds$ VERSUS $dx_a/ds$. Currently some courts, such as those in *Microsoft* and *Visa*, find defendants liable without requiring a showing that there has been significant harm to either consumers or to competition. Instead, they have found defendants liable based only on evidence that some harm to competitors has resulted, from which harm to the competitive process and consumers is inferred. Such a minimal standard provides no meaningful test of whether behavior is in fact anticompetitive, and the standard is thus almost certain to result in high probabilities of false convictions (high $x_c$). Moving to a stricter standard is likely to significantly decrease false convictions without nearly as significant a decrease in false acquittals.

To properly infer substantial consumer harm from harm to competitors, the courts must require plaintiffs to show that competitors have been harmed *significantly*—that is, there must be a significant effect on the competitors' ability to compete effectively. In addition the courts should require plaintiffs to show that competition or consumer welfare has been harmed *significantly* as a result of competitor harm—that is, that other competitors cannot in effect replace the harmed firm or firms. Without this more stringent standard the courts have no meaningful basis for distinguishing between procompetitive and anticompetitive behavior. Requiring such a standard would significantly reduce the probability of false convictions.

This stricter standard for consumer harm would have a much smaller impact on the probability of false acquittals. As we describe in more detail in discussing *Microsoft* and *Visa*, whether a challenged act causes or is likely to cause significant consumer harm is a question of fact, which can be addressed empirically. Those cases demonstrate likely judicial error resulting from a weak consumer harm standard; they provide support for the assertion that $x_c$ is currently high. But regardless of whether we are right on the merits, our discussion also illustrates that there were analyses the government could have undertaken in those cases that could have determined the existence and importance of consumer harm—and that the courts should have required. A stricter standard of consumer harm certainly requires more effort on the part of plaintiffs to prove liability, but it would not necessarily entail a significant increase in false acquittals.[34]

The minimal standard used by some courts would only be appropriate if there were strong reasons to believe that the vast majority of defendants had behaved anticompetitively (that $p$ is high) or that the costs resulting from false acquittals greatly outweighed the costs of false convictions (that $c_a$ is much higher than $c_c$) or both. Neither presumption seems warranted.

PROPORTION OF INNOCENCE VERSUS GUILT: $(1 - p)$ VERSUS $p$. While it is difficult to offer firm conclusions about the percentage of antitrust

---

34. Any extra resources the government would have to expend would be worthwhile from a social perspective in avoiding false acquittals. In addition, especially in cases such as the ones discussed here, it is doubtful that the additional cost of undertaking the analyses would represent a substantial increase in total costs.

defendants that have in fact caused consumer harm, there is little reason to believe it is so high as to justify a weak consumer harm standard. First, a weak standard would encourage some plaintiffs, particularly competitors, to file meritless suits seeking treble damages or the hobbling of an aggressive rival or both. Where plaintiffs do not have to show significant harm to competition or consumers, they can prevail in cases where no such harm exists. Thus it is reasonable to expect that under a weak consumer harm standard a significant proportion of private antitrust cases and perhaps even some government cases would target behavior that plaintiffs knew involved no consumer harm.

This problem is magnified because the antitrust case law considers suspect some business practices that are not generally anticompetitive. As the Chicago School of Economics has emphasized, there are various procompetitive reasons for firms to engage in many of the types of conduct that are frequently challenged under the Sherman Act, especially tying arrangements and vertical agreements among firms.[35] For example, companies may enter into exclusivity agreements to limit free-riding and opportunistic behavior or they may engage in tying or integration because of consumer preference or savings in transactions costs. The post-Chicago studies, while embracing the Chicago School's use of economics to evaluate the effect of allegedly anticompetitive practices on consumers, have identified many possible exceptions to its findings. These studies, for example, have identified conditions under which exclusivity restrictions or tying can be anticompetitive.[36] The models, however, require very specific conditions to hold, and they provide no support for the view enshrined in the case law that anticompetitive effects *generally* follow from exclusivity agreements or tying arrangements.[37] As Michael Whinston, one of the main contributors to this body of studies, has observed: "What is striking about the area of exclusive contracts and tying . . . is how little the current literature tells us about what [the typical effects on competition] are likely to be."[38]

If we are thus in a world where we cannot be confident that most antitrust defendants are guilty, there is no reason to rely on a standard of minimal consumer harm, especially when a more stringent standard incurs relatively low costs of false acquittals.

35. See, for example, Bork (1978, especially chaps. 14, 19).
36. See Whinston (1990); Carlton and Waldman (2002).
37. Hylton and Salinger (2001).
38. Whinston (2001, p. 79).

COSTS OF ERROR: $c_c$ VERSUS $c_a$. The cost of false acquittals depends on the extent of consumer harm from anticompetitive behavior. Assuming an act is anticompetitive, market forces may provide a correction in the longer run even when a court has failed to prohibit the act, but market forces are probably less effective in correcting judicial errors. As Judge Frank Easterbrook wrote, "the economic system corrects monopoly more readily than it corrects judicial errors. There is no automatic way to expunge mistaken decisions of the Supreme Court. A practice once condemned is likely to stay condemned, no matter its benefits. A monopolistic practice wrongly excused will eventually yield to competition, though, as the monopolist's higher prices attract rivalry."[39] For example, if a firm has achieved a monopoly over distribution through anticompetitive behavior, its competitors still have strong incentives to find alternative means of distributing their products. Market forces will certainly not correct all harms flowing from anticompetitive behavior, especially in the short run, but they can offset some of the anticompetitive effects in the long run.[40]

When courts mistakenly prohibit behavior that is procompetitive, however, market forces are prevented to some extent from serving as offsets. Competition is directly reduced in the market or markets at issue, and production and transaction costs may be increased. Moreover, procompetitive behavior is discouraged in other markets as companies across the economy seek to reduce their legal risk.

It is also important to note that the consequences of an antitrust conviction often go well beyond damage awards and orders to cease the offending behavior—though as our later discussion of *Visa* indicates, simple orders to cease and desist can have profound implications for industry structure and behavior. Courts can impose and have imposed a wide variety of behavioral restrictions and structural changes in attempts to remedy the effects of past actions that have been found illegal and to prevent future violations. Such broad remedies may have diverse consequences for competition and consumer welfare, many of which are unintended and unanticipated. The proclivity of courts to impose broad remedies in section 2 cases adds substantially to the expected societal cost of a finding of guilt where there is no real consumer harm.

---

39. Easterbrook (1984, p. 15).

40. For example, Crandall and Elzinga (forthcoming) examine the effectiveness of antitrust remedies and show that in some cases new entry made remedies irrelevant.

Thus the remedial effect of market forces for injunctions that are wrongly denied may limit the cost of false acquittals $(c_a)$ more than the cost of false convictions $(c_c)$, and the tendency of courts to impose broad remedies usually increases the number of false convictions. The larger $c_c$ is relative to $c_a$, all else equal, the more stringent should be the consumer harm standard required to find an antitrust violation.

### Additional Considerations

The standard of proof of substantial consumer harm that should be required also depends on other factors. Based on an error-cost analysis, our conclusion is that the courts should require a lower standard of proof when the practice at issue is one that the courts and economists have experience with in assessing competitive consequences. For example, simple horizontal price-fixing cases are treated under a *per se* standard because there is no dispute that the practice is harmful. Moreover, the costs of false convictions under that standard are minimal.[41] A price-fixing agreement between two companies without market power may not cause any significant consumer harm, but there is little cost in prohibiting such conduct. The Supreme Court in *Broadcast Music* v. *CBS*, however, chose not to apply the per se standard because there was a significant chance that, as the Court ultimately ruled under a rule-of-reason analysis, the price agreements in the case had significant procompetitive benefits.[42] This suggests that generally the courts should require a higher standard of proof when the issues in the case are complicated or novel. Greater evidence of consumer harm should be required when, for example, the plaintiff's liability theory depends on new and untested economic theories.

Another important factor is the likely impact of the relief demanded. When the plaintiff is seeking relief that is likely to have substantial external effects, such as companywide or industrywide restructuring, the court should require greater evidence of substantial consumer harm. Economics

41. Because Bork [note 15] finds us unclear on price fixing and horizontal mergers, a few additional remarks are in order. For the reasons just given in the text, we do *not* believe that direct (or indirect) proof of consumer harm should be required in *simple* price-fixing cases. However, evidence bearing on consumer harm is routinely and properly considered in horizontal merger cases: the Antitrust Division of the Department of Justice and the Federal Trade Commission examine whether the proposed merger will result in a significant increase in price or harm consumers in other ways. Only if there is a showing that consumer harm is likely is a defendant in a merger case obliged to prove efficiencies.

42. *Broadcast Music, Inc.* v. *CBS*, 441 U.S. 1 (1979).

provides good reason to believe that even in the presence of market power, firms and industries are organized efficiently because market forces tend to reward efficiency and punish inefficiency.[43] Thus any forced reorganization is likely to involve significant social costs. When the impact of relief extends beyond the challenged practice, we should be particularly certain that there is consumer harm that needs to be remedied. This is consistent with the point made by the appeals court decision in *Microsoft* that although the court had used a minimal standard for causation (whether Microsoft's actions had actually led to consumer harm) in its finding of liability, much greater judicial scrutiny of consumer harm, among other things, was needed to support the divestiture proposal accepted by the trial court:

> Divestiture is a remedy that is imposed only with great caution, in part because its long-term efficacy is rarely certain. Absent some measure of confidence that there has been an actual loss to competition that needs to be restored, wisdom counsels against adopting radical structural relief. . . . If the court on remand is unconvinced of the causal connection between Microsoft's exclusionary conduct and the company's position in the OS [operating systems] market, it may well conclude that divestiture is not an appropriate remedy.[44]

Clearly, relief need not be narrowly structural to have the sort of radical consequences that gave the appeals court pause. Indeed, as we discuss later, even what might seem to be simple cease-and-desist orders can have such consequences. Because there is no such thing as a harmless remedy, and no court is likely knowingly to impose a remedy with *de minimis* effects, serious direct or indirect evidence of *significant* consumer harm should be required to support a finding of liability.

## Microsoft

The Department of Justice filed its complaint against Microsoft in May 1998, focusing on the company's reaction to perceived threats to its Windows operating system, specifically from the Netscape Navigator Web browser and Sun Microsystems's Java technologies. In particular, the Justice

---

43. This presumption would therefore not necessarily hold in heavily regulated industries.
44. *United States* v. *Microsoft*, 253 F.3d 34, 80 (2001).

Department argued that Microsoft took steps to prevent Navigator from becoming a viable platform that could compete with Windows. The department made four broad allegations: market foreclosure and tying under section 1 of the Sherman Act, and attempted monopolization and monopoly maintenance under section 2.[45] Twenty states and the District of Columbia joined in these claims and also asserted Microsoft engaged in monopoly leveraging in violation of section 2 of the Sherman Act.[46] The district court judge dismissed the monopoly leveraging claim before the start of the trial and rejected the section 1 foreclosure claim as well as several of the charges included under the section 2 monopoly maintenance claims. But the judge found Microsoft liable for tying under section 1 and many of the claims under section 2.[47] He ordered a remedy that included splitting Microsoft into two separate companies.

Microsoft appealed the district court's liability findings to the District of Columbia Circuit Court of Appeals, which reversed the section 2 attempted monopolization claim, affirmed a portion of the section 2 monopoly maintenance claim, and vacated and remanded the section 1 tying claims. The appeals court vacated the remedies ordered by the district court in their entirety and remanded them for the district court "to determine the propriety of a specific remedy for the limited ground of liability which we have upheld."[48]

In September 2001 the Justice Department and the state plaintiffs announced that they would not pursue the tying claims on remand. In November 2001 Microsoft settled the case with the department and nine

---

45. Complaint, *United States* v. *Microsoft*, Civil Action No. 98-1232 (TPJ), May 18, 1998 (www.usdoj.gov/atr/cases/f1700/1763.htm [December 3, 2002]).

46. Plaintiff States' First Amended Complaint, *New York* v. *Microsoft Corp.*, Civil Action No. 98-1233 (TPJ), July 17, 1998, paras. 91–92.

47. Conclusions of Law, *United States* v. *Microsoft*, Civil Action Nos. 98-1232 and 98-1233 (TPJ), April. 3, 2000.

48. *United States* v. *Microsoft Corp.*, 253 F.3d 34, 107 (2001). Bork's characterization of Microsoft's behavior goes far beyond the courts' findings in many important respects. For example, he refers to "Microsoft's foreclosure of the distribution of Navigator" (p. 53), though this charge was explicitly rejected by the district court. See Conclusions of Law, *United States* v. *Microsoft*, Civil Action Nos. 98-1232 and 98-1233 (TPJ), 2, 38, April 3, 2000; *United States* v. *Microsoft*, 253 F.3d 34, 70 (2001). And he describes Microsoft's conduct as "predatory" throughout, even though there was no finding of predation by the court of appeals, and in oral argument the government explicitly denied that it was charging predation. See Transcript, *Microsoft* v. *United States* and *Microsoft* v. *State of New York*, United States Court of Appeals for the D.C. Circuit, 79, Nos. 00-5212 and 00-5213 (February 26, 2001); *United States* v. *Microsoft*, 253 F.3d 34, 68 (2001). Other examples are easily found.

of the state plaintiffs.[49] That settlement had to be approved by a new district court judge. Meanwhile, the nine remaining state plaintiffs and the District of Columbia pursued stricter remedies before the same district court judge that reviewed the settlement.[50] After a Tunney Act proceeding to review whether the settlement agreement was in the public interest and an evidentiary hearing concerning an alternative remedy proposed by the nine litigating states, Judge Colleen Kollar-Kotelly adopted with minor modifications the remedy embodied in the settlement agreement.

### Consumer Harm

Although the appeals court stated the appropriate principles for establishing significant consumer harm, it did not require the government to provide evidence that demonstrated the existence of such harm. The government argued that Microsoft had prevented Netscape from developing into a competing platform competitor. The government did not, however, provide any evidence or analyses that showed that the anticompetitive acts at issue had harmed Netscape as a potential platform or that Netscape seriously planned to become a platform competitor.

LIABILITY STANDARD. The appeals court stated the standard on liability:

> The question in this case is not whether Java or Navigator would actually have developed into viable platform substitutes, but (1) whether as a general matter the exclusion of nascent threats is the type of conduct that is reasonably capable of contributing significantly to a defendant's continued monopoly power and (2) whether Java and Navigator reasonably constituted nascent threats at the time Microsoft engaged in the anticompetitive conduct at issue.[51]

We believe the appeals court stated the right principles for its liability standard but failed to apply them correctly. First, in finding liability, the court relied on the district court's findings that Navigator had been

49. Revised Proposed Final Judgment, *United States* v. *Microsoft*, Civil Action Nos. 98-1232 and 98-1233, November 6, 2002.

50. Two of the original twenty state plaintiffs had dropped out by this stage. One state, South Carolina, withdrew its complaint in December 1998 when America Online announced it would purchase Netscape. New Mexico had already reached a settlement with Microsoft in July 2001. Hahn and Layne-Farrar (forthcoming).

51. *United States* v. *Microsoft Corp*, 253 F.3d 34, 79 (2001).

significantly harmed by those Microsoft actions the appeals court found anticompetitive ("anticompetitive acts") and that Navigator was a "nascent" competitor to Windows.[52] However, the district court's finding of harm to Navigator had been based on the entire set of acts it found anticompetitive. The appeals court subsequently narrowed the acts it upheld as anticompetitive, stating it had "drastically altered the District Court's conclusions on liability."[53] A reassessment of the finding of substantial harm to Navigator was necessary to determine if the remaining anticompetitive acts had caused significant harm to it as a nascent competitor to Windows. But as we discuss next there were empirical analyses that could have been performed and would have addressed whether the challenged actions by Microsoft had caused any significant harm to Navigator.[54]

Second, the appeals court described its liability standard as "edentulous" because it did not require a showing that Java or Navigator would have actually developed as platform competitors, but it appeared to believe that its toothless standard was unavoidable given the nascent character of the competitive threats.[55] It did not want to permit harm to a nascent competitor simply because such an entity, by definition, would not yet be an established competitor. The appeals court reasoned that "to some degree, 'the defendant is made to suffer the uncertain consequences of its own undesirable conduct.'"[56] Although determining whether a company is really a nascent threat is not easy, the courts should nevertheless require an assessment based on the available evidence of whether a firm that is harmed "reasonably constituted" (as the court put it) a nascent threat. The court's failure to require this made the liability standard weaker in practice than in the principles asserted by the court.

---

52. For convenience, we refer to the acts found anticompetitive by the appeals court as the "anticompetitive acts." However, closer examination suggests that there was no showing of significant consumer harm and that the acts should not be characterized as anticompetitive.

53. *United States* v. *Microsoft*, 253 F.3d 34, 105 (2001).

54. The plaintiffs would, however, have had difficulty on remand for a different reason. In rejecting the attempted monopolization claim, the appeals court found that the plaintiffs had not proved the existence of a browser market protected by barriers to entry and found that they would not have another opportunity to prove the existence of this market on remand. Without such a market, there is no context for evaluating the competitive significance of actions Microsoft took toward Netscape. *United States* v. *Microsoft*, 253 F.3d 34, 81-83 (2001). See also Fox (2002, pp. 386–87).

55. *United States* v. *Microsoft*, 79.

56. Philip E. Areeda and Herbert Hovenkamp, *Antitrust Law*, vol. 3 (Little, Brown, 1996), p. 78, quoted in *United States* v. *Microsoft*, 79.

HARM TO COMPETITORS. The core theory of the plaintiffs' case during the liability phase was that Microsoft's actions caused Navigator to lose the ubiquity it needed to become a platform competitor to Windows.[57] The plaintiffs argued that although Navigator was not an operating system competitor to Windows at that time, it could develop into a platform competitor. If Navigator were to achieve ubiquity, the argument went, software firms might write to application programming interfaces (APIs) that Navigator might develop and expose, rather than to Windows APIs. The plaintiffs argued that Navigator might thus eventually become a platform competitor to Windows.

The plaintiffs' expert, Franklin Fisher, had suggested that the minimum threshold share Navigator needed for ubiquity was 50 percent.[58] Navigator's usage share had fallen to less than 15 percent by the time of the remedies hearing (though it was substantially higher at the time of trial).[59] So a central question for liability should have been whether the acts found anticompetitive by the appeals court were likely to have reduced Navigator's share by more than 35 percentage points.[60] Of course, that question would seem to have antitrust meaning only if there is an antitrust market for browsers; otherwise there is no numeraire for calculating a share. But the appeals court found that the plaintiffs had failed to prove a browser market and could not get a second bite at that apple on remand.[61]

Assuming that browsers constitute a relevant market, however, one cannot determine from the trial record whether the actions found anticompetitive by the appellate court prevented Netscape from achieving

---

57. There was a similar claim regarding Java. Microsoft presented similar evidence during the remedies stage arguing that, as with Navigator, Microsoft's actions did not affect Java significantly enough to harm competition. For the purposes of this paper, we focus on Microsoft's actions that related to Navigator.

58. Transcript of Trial: Oral Rebuttal Testimony of Franklin Fisher (vol. 33, PM Session), *United States* v. *Microsoft*, Civil Action No. 98-1232 and 98-1223, January 6, 1999, 35.

59. Direct Testimony of Kevin M. Murphy, *New York* v. *Microsoft Corp.*, Civil Action No. 98-1233 (CKK), April 12, 2002, para. 38.

60. Because the appeals court reduced the number of acts found anticompetitive, a reexamination of liability would need to determine whether the remaining anticompetitive acts had caused significant harm to Navigator as a competitor to Windows. Such a hearing would have presumably taken place about the time the remedies hearing actually took place. This chapter discusses the analyses presented by Murphy at the remedies hearing. Most of Murphy's analyses relied on data that would have been available around the time of the initial trial.

61. See note 54.

Fisher's ubiquity threshold. Many of the important actions taken by Microsoft in competing with Navigator were found not to be anticompetitive. Some actions were found permissible by the district court; others, initially found anticompetitive by the district court, were later ruled permissible by the appellate court.[62] Some of the more significant Microsoft actions found permissible were: (1) offering its Internet Explorer at no additional cost to consumers, (2) investing heavily in improving the quality of Explorer, (3) making it free for internet access providers, (4) offering payments to access providers for distributing Explorer, (5) developing and distributing at no charge a "tool" enabling access providers to customize Explorer, and (6) designing Explorer in a "componentized" way that made it attractive to AOL and other partners.[63]

The relevant question is whether Navigator's loss of ubiquity could be plausibly attributed to the remaining anticompetitive acts rather than to the large set of competitive acts found to be legal. If, for example, Microsoft's anticompetitive acts had reduced Navigator's share by 5 percentage points, Navigator's share would still only be 20 percent and those anticompetitive acts would not have significantly harmed its ability to become a platform competitor. That is, even if Microsoft's suspect actions did harm Navigator's success as a browser, they may have had no significant effect on its ability to develop into a platform competitor. To find liability without real evidence of the likelihood of significant harm to competition or consumers is to move very close to a per se standard, which seems unjustifiable for the types of practices at issue.

The appeals court's decision failed to require any evidence that would have shown whether Microsoft's actions, individually or collectively, denied

---

62. Memorandum Opinion, *State of New York, et al.* v. *Microsoft,* Civil Action No. 98-1233 (CKK) November 1, 2002, 18–25. See also Evans (2002). Bork simply ignores this and asserts that "Netscape's browser was driven from the market by nonefficient exclusionary practices" (p. 62). Neither the district court nor the appeals court made such a finding. See Conclusions of Law, *United States* v. *Microsoft,* Civil Action Nos. 98-1232 and 98-1233, 2, 38 (TPJ, April 3, 2000); *United States* v. *Microsoft,* 253 F.3d 34, 70–71 (2001). We believe that if this had actually been proven, it would have been quite simple to show that consumers were harmed.

63. The appeals court reversed the district court's initial finding of liability on (3), (4), and (5). The district court was ambiguous on whether (1) and (2) were anticompetitive, but the appeals court found that they were clearly permissible. *State of New York, et al.* v. *Microsoft,* 3. Making Internet Explorer "componentized" allowed other companies such as AOL to include its functionality in their own software, without necessarily opening an Explorer window, so that consumers might not even know they were using Explorer functionality. This had both technical and marketing advantages for potential partners. Direct Testimony of Kevin M. Murphy, *New York* v. *Microsoft Corp.,* Civil Action No. 98-1233 (CKK), April 12, 2002, paras. 50, 108–109, 117.

Navigator the ubiquity it needed as a platform competitor. For example, consider the appeals court finding that Microsoft's contractual terms with original equipment manufacturers (OEMs) that prohibited the deletion of the Internet Explorer icon from the desktop or the start menu was an anti-competitive act.[64] It stated that by "preventing OEMs from removing visible means of user access to IE, the license restriction prevents many OEMs from pre-installing a rival browser, and, therefore, protects Microsoft's monopoly from the competition that middleware might otherwise present." The court relied on the district court's finding that "OEMs cannot practically install a second browser in addition to IE, the court found, in part because 'pre-installing more than one product in a given category . . . can significantly increase an OEM's support costs, for the redundancy can lead to confusion among novice users.'"[65] The appeals court found that there were no procompetitive justifications and concluded that the restriction was anticompetitive. The district court did not cite any evidence or analysis that showed this restriction actually had a significant effect on Navigator.[66] The appeals court failed to apply its own test of whether this restriction was "reasonably capable of contributing significantly" to the maintenance of Microsoft's market power in finding that this restriction, by itself, constituted a violation of the Sherman Act.

Kevin Murphy, Microsoft's expert at the remedies hearing, testified that this question could be addressed empirically. He examined both the individual and collective impact on Navigator use from the alleged anticompetitive acts and argued that together they affected Navigator's decline by "no more than a few percentage points."[67] For example, he considered the effect of the "no removal" restriction, as well as restrictions on the promotion of third-party browsers or Internet access providers through the use of unusually shaped icons, in one of his analyses. Murphy compared Navigator use among a control group of Internet users whose browser choice was unlikely to be affected by these restriction and a treatment group whose choice of a browser might have been affected. The difference would

64. *United States* v. *Microsoft*, 253 F.3d 34, 61 (2001).

65. *United States* v. *Microsoft*, Civil Action Nos. 98-1232 and 98-1233 (TPJ), Findings of Fact (November 5, 1999), 159, quoted in *United States* v. *Microsoft*, 61.

66. Direct Testimony of Kevin M. Murphy, *New York* v. *Microsoft Corp.*, Civil Action No. 98-1233 (CKK), April 12, 2002.

67. Testimony of Kevin M. Murphy, *New York* v. *Microsoft*, para. 92. Richard Schmalensee's testimony at trial provided similar findings regarding the lack of effect of various contested Microsoft actions.

measure the collective impact of the anticompetitive acts on the distribution or use of Netscape's browser. Using two data sources, he found that there was an insignificant difference in Navigator's decline between the treatment and the control group.[68]

Another of Murphy's analyses considered the change in the use of Navigator for subscribers to two groups of service providers: the treatment group of providers that signed contracts containing terms upheld as anticompetitive by the appeals court; and a control group of providers that signed less restrictive agreements containing no illegal terms. Navigator's share loss was essentially the same for both groups, thus indicating an insignificant incremental impact from the terms in the providers' contracts that the appeals court condemned.

The litigating states offered no substantive rebuttal to Murphy's testimony.[69] Regardless of the merits, however, we want to emphasize that this is a question that the appeals court should have required the district court to address directly before a final determination of liability, especially in light of the appeals court's "drastic" modifications to the trial court's liability findings.[70] This was a question that was susceptible to empirical examination, as Murphy's testimony demonstrated. Instead, the appeals court simply assumed that each of Microsoft's challenged actions that it did not

---

68. Direct Testimony of Kevin M. Murphy, *New York* v. *Microsoft*, paras. 58–67. The first comparison was between Navigator use by Internet technology professionals ("unlikely to be constrained by the anticompetitive acts because they are technically sophisticated, knowledgeable and can easily and cheaply acquire whatever brand of browser they wish") and Navigator use generally (which could have been affected by the anticompetitive acts). The second comparison was between use by people working in medium or large businesses or the government (whose "'choice' of browser for these users is often determined by the software configuration installed and supported by their employer") and use by those at home or working in small businesses (who were more likely to be affected by the anticompetitive acts).

69. The litigating states' economic expert, Carl Shapiro, stated that "the Findings of Fact and the Court of Appeals decision in this case make it very clear that Microsoft's illegal conduct had significant effects on Netscape Navigator and on Sun's Java platform." Direct Testimony of Carl Shapiro, *New York* v. *Microsoft Corp.*, Civil Action No. 98-1233 (CKK), April 5, 2002, paras. 60–61. Shapiro did not address the issues Murphy discussed in this testimony. The litigating states had the option to call Shapiro to provide rebuttal testimony but chose not to. The trial court dismissed his analysis of causation issues, commenting that "Dr. Shapiro does not appear to have gathered or synthesized empirical information or to have applied particular economic principles." See Memorandum Opinion, *State of New York, et al.* v. *Microsoft*, Civil Action No. 98-1233 (CKK) November 1, 2002, 116.

70. At trial the government presented some analyses of the impact on Navigator use of some of Microsoft's contractual restrictions, but this included restrictions that were ultimately found permissible. It is thus not possible to use the government's analysis to estimate the effects of the anticompetitive acts affirmed by the appeals court.

find legal had sufficiently reduced Navigator's potential ability to compete with Windows so as to injure competition and thus harm consumers.[71]

HARM TO COMPETITION. The appeals court decision also suffered from a second major flaw. Although the court asked the right question, "whether Java and Navigator reasonably constituted nascent threats at the time Microsoft engaged in the anticompetitive conduct at issue," it accepted the district court's findings that Navigator was a nascent threat. The district court's findings were based on general concerns expressed by Microsoft executives about the threat from Navigator but did not include specific evidence indicating that Navigator would have (or could have) developed into a platform competitor even with the necessary ubiquity.[72] Microsoft had been worried that Netscape would transform Navigator into a competing platform.[73] But there is little evidence from either the trial or intensive interviews with Netscape employees conducted by Michael Cusumano

71. The trial court rejected Murphy's causation analysis: "Still, Dr. Murphy's conclusion that the anticompetitive conduct identified in this case had *no* effect upon Microsoft's monopoly can be seen to undercut, if not directly contradict, the inference of causation necessary to the appellate court's imposition of liability. . . . Most troubling to the Court in examining Dr. Murphy's analysis is the fact that many of the conclusions reached by Dr. Murphy cannot be reconciled logically with significant portions of the appellate court's opinion." See Memorandum Opinion, *State of New York, et al.* v. *Microsoft*, Civil Action No. 98-1233 (CKK) November 1, 2002, 118. The difficulty is that the appeals court's opinion is internally inconsistent and cannot be reconciled with its own findings or with the trial record. As Eleanor Fox has observed, after enunciating a tough test for determining whether exclusion reduced social welfare, "the court shifted to a loose analysis wherein foreclosure became the touchstone for 'anticompetitive.' Foreclosure of unspecified dimensions from one important route of access to the browser market (although plaintiffs had failed to prove a browser market) was accepted as "anticompetitive" and thus sufficient for the Government's prima facie case." Fox (2002, p. 387). See also note 6 on p. 50.

72. Bork argues that Microsoft's decision to compete aggressively with Netscape establishes that it faced no other competitors: "No predator would attack particular firms if other firms, unaffected by the onslaught, remained to offer competition" (p. 52). Of course firms compete aggressively all the time in real-world markets and it leads to vigorous competition that helps consumers. He characterizes Microsoft's actions as predatory based on its internal communications. This amounts to basing market definition on e-mails, perhaps supplemented by linguistic arguments on the labeling of particular competitive actions.

73. If there were clear evidence that a defendant believed another firm was a potential competitor and if the defendant took anticompetitive actions that eliminated that other firm, liability might be appropriate even if it turned out that the other firm was not actually a potential competitor. That is, a defendant should presumably not escape liability if it took anticompetitive actions that eliminated a firm it clearly believed was a potential competitor simply because its belief was mistaken. However, it is notoriously difficult to assess the beliefs and intent of an organization, and it is generally preferable to examine directly the extent to which a firm actually was a potential competitor. At the very least, such an examination will shed light on the plausibility of the beliefs the defendant is alleged to have

and David Yoffie that Netscape ever seriously planned to do so.[74] James Barksdale (Netscape's CEO), for example, suggested in trial testimony that the comment by Marc Andreessen (cofounder of Netscape and an early developer of browser software) about reducing the role of Windows to that of providing "slightly buggy device drivers" reflected his youth and a "spirit of jocularity and sometimes sarcasm that have gotten us in trouble."[75] Barksdale also testified that Microsoft had "never maintained in a serious way that [Navigator] could substitute for all [of the platform characteristics of Windows]."[76] We are not suggesting that the plaintiffs should have had to, in the appeals court's words, "confidently reconstruct a product's hypothetical technological development."[77] However, at a minimum the government should have had to demonstrate that its theory regarding the Navigator threat was supported by the available evidence.

The plaintiffs' theory at trial was that, over time and with ubiquity, Navigator could have perhaps developed application programming interfaces that would attract software developers. But the plaintiffs presented no evidence that Netscape had ever taken any significant steps to develop Navigator as a platform. During the remedies phase Murphy testified that the decisions made by Netscape and later AOL indicated they had no plans to develop Navigator as a platform competitor.[78] (The litigating state plaintiffs offered no substantive rebuttal to this testimony.) For example, a June 1998 strategy briefing "made it clear that the company's server products

---

held. (Bork does not address the issues raised here in his apparent criticism of us, stating: "If the predator intended to kill a victim in order to harm consumers, the fact that the victim was killed due to a misapprehension by the predator should surely not be a defense" [p. 62].) The issue Murphy was addressing—whether broad remedial relief was needed to restore lost competition—is different and should turn on whether an eliminated firm was actually likely to have become a competitor, not on any mistaken beliefs of the defendant.

74. Cusumano and Yoffie (2000).

75. Transcript of Trial: Oral Testimony of James Barksdale (vol. 2, PM Session), *United States* v. *Microsoft*, Civil Action Nos. 98-1232 and 98-1223, October 20, 1998, 73.

76. Transcript of Trial: Oral Testimony of James Barksdale, *United States* v. *Microsoft*, 73.

77. *United States* v. *Microsoft*, 253 F.3d 34, 79 (2001). Bork argues that it would be legitimate to find a violation even assuming "that Microsoft's attack proved not to be the real reason for the disappearance of Netscape Navigator" because the result "would be only an injunction that proved unnecessary against illegal practices" (p. 62). But the federal and state governments sought more than bare-bones injunctive relief. The district court ordered far more; and in negotiations, after the case was remanded, Microsoft agreed to more. The notion that relief in a real section 2 case can ever be harmless to a losing defendant seems far-fetched.

78. Direct Testimony of Kevin M. Murphy, *New York* v. *Microsoft Corp.*, Civil Action No. 98-1233 (CKK), April 12, 2002, paras. 107–24.

had replaced the browser as the heart of Netscape's product plans."[79] Consistent with this focus, Netscape and AOL have not developed the types of application programming interfaces (APIs) that software developers would need to start using Navigator as a platform instead of Windows.[80] Even today AOL uses Internet Explorer, not Navigator, to provide browsing functionality.[81]

Murphy noted that, by contrast, if Netscape and later AOL had serious plans to develop Navigator into a platform competitor, we would expect them to have taken very different actions.[82] They would have made much more significant efforts to develop APIs for Navigator and would have made Navigator more componentized and thus easier for potential partners to use, as had been urged by IBM/Lotus, Intuit, and AOL (before AOL acquired Netscape).[83] One would also expect that Netscape and AOL would have made more effort to pay for wider distribution of Navigator, or at least use it in AOL's client software, in light of the potential revenues from developing it as a platform competitor.

Again, although we believe the evidence suggests that Microsoft's anticompetitive acts did not deny Navigator the ubiquity the plaintiffs argued it needed and there was no evidence that Navigator had a significant chance to develop as a platform competitor, the point to emphasize is that those are factual issues that could and should have been examined at the liability stage. Instead, the district and appeals courts, using a weak consumer harm standard, accepted a liability case presented by the plaintiffs that did not attempt to assess either the extent to which Navigator had been harmed or the extent to which any harm to Navigator was important to competition in the relevant market. We are not suggesting here that a plaintiff should be required to show the exact path competition would have taken in the absence of the allegedly anticompetitive acts, especially when the case involves companies that are allegedly nascent competitors. Rather, when claims of harm to competitors and to competition can be examined

79. Cusumano and Yoffie (2000), cited in Direct Testimony of Kevin M. Murphy, *New York* v. *Microsoft Corp.*, Civil Action No. 98-1233 (CKK), April 12, 2002, para. 107.

80. Murphy's testimony indicated that only a handful of APIs have been developed for Navigator and that most of those do not provide the type of functionality across operating systems that has been argued might make Navigator attractive as a platform.

81. There are reports that there is beta testing of a version of AOL's client software that relies on Navigator's browsing code. Jim Hu, "AOL Launches New Netscape Browser," *ZDNet News*, August 29, 2002. See http://zdnet.com.com/2102-1104-955850.html (December 3, 2002).

82. Direct Testimony of Kevin M. Murphy, *New York* v. *Microsoft*, paras. 123–24.

83. Direct Testimony of Kevin M. Murphy, *New York* v. *Microsoft*, paras. 109, 117.

to determine whether the potential harms are significant and realistic, that inquiry must be undertaken. As in the analysis of postpredation recoupment under the *Brooke Group* test, the plaintiff should be required to show the plausibility of the scenarios it puts forward, not to prove beyond a doubt the correctness of any one of them.

## Visa and MasterCard

Payment card systems have historically consisted of companies in two groups: proprietary systems and open systems. Of the four largest systems in the United States, American Express and Discover are proprietary systems, Visa and MasterCard are open systems. The proprietary systems, American Express and Discover, solicit cardholders to use the systems' charge and credit cards and acquire merchants (or contract with others to acquire merchants). A proprietary system operates the necessary processing infrastructure, conducts advertising and other marketing activities, and performs research and development. It determines the prices and other terms and conditions for its cardholders and merchants and retains the profits from its activities.

Visa and MasterCard, the open systems, are run as not-for-profit cooperatives or associations. The cooperative provides its members with a range of services. It runs the processing infrastructure, manages the brand, and engages in system-level research and development. It also provides rules that members must follow. The cooperative operates on a not-for-profit basis, setting member fees at a level that is expected to cover system costs (including funds for working capital and contingencies). It does not set prices to cardholders or merchants.[84] Individual members solicit cardholders and merchants, set prices and other terms and conditions, process transactions (sometimes with the assistance of third-party processors), advertise and establish the brand image for their cards, and develop and implement card features.[85]

Two central issues concerned the government in the investigation that led up to *United States* v. *Visa*. The first was the absence of any Visa or

---

84. The court found that Visa and MasterCard both operated on a not-for-profit basis. *United States* v. *Visa*, 163 F. Supp.2d 332 (2001). MasterCard completed its reorganization as a stock rather than a membership corporation on July 1, 2002. It is unclear whether this will affect its not-for-profit operation. Visa continues to operate on a not-for-profit basis and set its system fees at cost.

85. Evans and Schmalensee (1999, p. 262).

MasterCard rules that prevented banks from being members of both systems, a situation commonly referred to as duality. In other words the government wanted *more* separation between Visa and MasterCard. The second was the existence of Visa and MasterCard rules that prohibited members from issuing American Express or Discover cards. In other words the government wanted *less* separation between Visa (or MasterCard) and American Express (or Discover).

The government told Visa that the association could not consistently defend these contradictory positions on membership. Visa told the government it could not consistently prosecute both duality and exclusivity as antitrust violations.[86] Nevertheless, duality and exclusivity became counts one and two of the government's case, and Visa and MasterCard mounted a defense on both counts. The government believed it had a way out of the contradictions. Through its economic expert, Michael Katz, it put forward a theory that one could distinguish between duality in governance and duality in issuance.[87] He argued that duality in governance (or overlapping governance generally) was anticompetitive and duality in issuance (or multiple issuance generally) was procompetitive. Thus he proposed to end dual governance without ending dual issuance. Further, the repeal of the exclusivity rules could then be viewed as an extension of (procompetitive) dual issuance to multiple issuance.

Visa had been opposed to duality at its inception in the late 1970s but as a small entity at that time had acquiesced in the face of potential antitrust liability and what it viewed as the unwillingness of the government to support its position against duality. Richard Schmalensee, Visa's economic expert, believed that having exclusive systems was best overall for system and issuer competition, although it was not clear the government had shown that dual governance (as opposed to duality in total) had led to

86. Two of this chapter's authors, Evans and Schmalensee, participated in discussions with the Justice Department during the three years that preceded the filing of the lawsuit. In his description of *Visa* Robert Bork completely ignores the duality count of the government's case, even though the tension between the duality and exclusivity counts was a central feature of the proceeding. And he does not seem to realize that the novelty and complexity of the industry's organizational structure—this is *not* a simple manufacturer/dealer case—means that labeling arguments are particularly unreliable substitutes for economic analysis of competitive and consumer impacts. For both these reasons Bork sees a simple, straightforward case with an obvious remedy while the government saw a complex situation requiring what they believed was a carefully crafted remedy. Bork provides not a summary of the case as brought and tried, but a summary of that portion of the district court's opinion that dealt with exclusivity.

87. We use the unmodified term "duality" to refer to duality as it now exists, encompassing duality in membership and in governance.

anticompetitive effects. Moreover, reacting to the value of loyalty, both Visa and MasterCard had taken steps to increase the extent to which issuers were dedicated to one system or the other, thus ameliorating some of the potential harm from duality.

In its decision the district court rejected the government's attempted distinction between dual governance and dual issuance. The court found some harmful effects from duality—that duality "has led to some blunting of competitive incentives," but could not ascribe the effects solely to dual governance.[88] The court found that dual governance was an artificial distinction that had no foundation in the actual operation of Visa and MasterCard and that large issuers could have an important influence on association decisions even if they were not governors.

The court reasoned that it could set aside its finding that duality, in total, resulted in "some blunting of competitive incentives" because the government's claim related only to dual governance, so that "whether or not dual issuance has been or will be the source of anticompetitive conduct is not the issue."[89] The question of whether dual or multiple issuance can be anticompetitive, however, is relevant to evaluation of the exclusivity rules. Visa sought to prohibit the extension of multiple issuance to American Express because, among other effects, the practice would blunt competitive incentives, as had happened with duality. The court failed to address the problem of blunted incentives in its assessment of procompetitive effects from the exclusivity rules.

As noted earlier, courts should be particularly careful to require clear evidence of consumer harm in a case involving a very complicated industry structure and a novel liability theory put forward by the plaintiff. The relief devised by the court ordered Visa and MasterCard to eliminate their exclusivity rules and rescinded the existing partnership agreements already signed by banks to allow them to sign agreements with American Express or Discover. (The government's proposed relief differed substantially from the court's because it had sought to address both the duality and exclusivity claims.) The court's relief could lead to dramatic changes in the structure of the payment card industry. The greater system separation that had come about in recent years through the action of Visa and MasterCard, noted with approval by the court, could be in large measure undone. In the face of potential industry restructuring and the court's own ambivalence

88. *United States* v. *Visa*, 163 F. Supp.2d 322, 363 (2001).
89. *United States* v. *Visa*, 163 F. Supp.2d 322, 329 (2001).

about the impact of decreased system separation, it should have been especially important to require the government to provide evidence on significant consumer harm that related to the remedy to be imposed. We believe the court failed to do this.

### Consumer Harm

The government's case on consumer harm fits into two categories. First, it contended that American Express had been harmed by the exclusivity rules and that the loss of system competition constituted consumer harm. (For convenience, we refer to American Express rather than both American Express and Discover.) Second, the government argued that cardholders were harmed by the loss of variety that would have been available if Visa or MasterCard members issued cards for American Express. The court accepted both arguments.[90]

The government's liability case on exclusivity contained the same two central flaws as in *Microsoft*. First, it made no attempt to assess the extent to which the competitor (in this case American Express) was harmed. Second, it made no attempt to demonstrate the extent to which the alleged harm to a competitor would harm competition. And, as in *Microsoft*, these were questions that could have been answered empirically. In accepting the government's case the district court failed to require a showing that Visa's exclusivity rules had caused significant harm to competition or consumers.

Visa offered procompetitive justifications for its exclusivity rule, although a full discussion is outside the scope of this chapter. The association argued that the rule was important for ensuring the loyalty of its members in furthering the growth of the cooperative. It also contended that the exclusivity rule limited the ability of its members to take opportunistic

---

90. Bork, again, apparently believes that the government tried to do more than it needed to. He argues that the exclusivity agreements were "of a sort familiar to antitrust law: a horizontal agreement among competitors to refuse to deal and thus not to compete by offering new brands to their customers" (p. 63). Having affixed this label on the basis of surface appearances—and shined it by arguing that the intent of the Visa and MasterCard banks' voting for exclusivity was anticompetitive—he would immediately shift the burden to defendants to show the agreement produced efficiencies. No analysis of effects on competitors, let alone on consumers, would be required, even though such analyses are frequently done. In unusual organizational structures or rapidly changing industries, however, efficiencies are difficult to prove—indeed, imagine trying to *prove* that all the familiar restrictions a law firm imposes on its partners enhance. Because it is hard to prove efficiencies, under Bork's approach if the defendant loses the labeling battle, the game is over even for practices that directly benefit consumers.

actions that would undermine the success of the cooperative. The court rejected these justifications.[91] Visa also argued that the exclusivity rule was procompetitive because it helped maintain separation between the Visa and American Express systems. The court rejected this argument without any detailed discussion and did not appear to recognize the inconsistency with its finding that duality had led to "some blunting of competitive incentives."[92]

### Harm to Competitors

The court found harm to American Express from the Visa and Master-Card exclusivity rules because they prevented American Express from taking actions it claimed to want to take. But the court did not require the government to assess the extent to which American Express had been weakened as a system competitor. Harm to a competitor, even an important one, does not imply harm to competition or to consumers.

The court found that "banks provide essential attributes to network competitors" because "Visa and MasterCard banks are the sources of virtually all of the expertise in issuing general purpose cards in the United States outside of American Express and Discover themselves."[93] There is no dispute that successful issuers have certain skills and specialized knowledge that are the reasons for their success, as is true in general with any successful company. The antitrust question, however, is how significantly American Express is harmed by not having access to these issuers.

It was unclear whether Visa and MasterCard's exclusivity rules prevented American Express from gaining access to important issuer skills—American Express is the largest card issuer in the United States and, with 20 percent of card volume, is only slightly smaller than MasterCard, a system with thousands of issuers and 26 percent of card volume.[94] American Express has managed to acquire the issuing skills necessary for that success without having had access to any Visa and MasterCard members. Historically American Express has chosen to operate as a single-issuer proprietary system.

---

91. *United States* v. *Visa*, 329. We believe the court erred in its findings, but a discussion of this issue is outside of the scope of this chapter.

92. *United States* v. *Visa*, 330, 363. The court briefly addressed the exclusivity rule as procompetitive in the introductory section of the decision and did not consider it in the detailed analysis of procompetitive justifications.

93. *United States* v. *Visa*, 389.

94. *United States* v. *Visa*, 341, 387.

Entry and expansion in the credit card issuing business also appears to be relatively easy. Many of the largest Visa and MasterCard issuers have entered or grown greatly in the past decade.[95] These new or previously minor issuers were able to develop the issuing skills to become major issuers quickly without gaining direct access to the skills of existing card issuers. Similarly, American Express could develop additional issuing skills or open up its system to new entrants in a relatively short time. The company might earn higher profits if it could gain immediate access to the issuing capabilities that Visa and MasterCard members have developed, but that does not mean it needs to do so to compete effectively. Moreover, it has a number of ways of getting access to existing issuer skills in the industry. It can contract with Visa and MasterCard members to provide any expertise it needs as long as they do not issue American Express cards. The company can even purchase and convert existing Visa and MasterCard portfolios, which it acknowledged after the trial it can do successfully in addition to purchasing issuer skills.[96]

There was no economic evidence that American Express, as a system competitor, suffered any significant cost disadvantages. Its CEO, Harvey Golub, testified that there would be at best only "marginal" (i.e., small) cost savings from additional volume.[97] Moreover, switching 6 percent of volume from MasterCard to American Express, thus reversing the size of the two systems, would simply transfer any scale economies from one system to the

95. *United States* v. *Visa*, 365.

96. American Express has, in fact, purchased bankcard portfolios, including Bank of Hawaii, BSB Bank & Trust, and Valley National Bank. See American Express Press Releases (http://home3. americanexpress.com/corp/latestnews/hawaii.asp; http://home3.americanexpress.com/corp/ latestnews/bsb-bank.asp; http://home3.americanexpress.com/corp/latestnews/shopright.asp. At trial American Express witnesses stated that purchasing portfolios was not an economically viable strategy. American Express has since directly contradicted that testimony by stating that it has successfully pursued that strategy with no significant problems. Opening Brief of Defendant-Appellant Visa U.S.A., Inc., *United States* v. *Visa*, 98 Civ. 7076 (BSJ), May 14, 2002, 41.

97. Trial Testimony of Harvey Golub, *United States* v. *Visa*, 98 Civ. 7076 (BSJ), July 5, 2000, 2770–71. The court cited testimony from Richard Schmalensee to support its statement that "since the card network services business is driven by scale, increasing the scale of American Express and Discover will reduce their costs and increase their competitive strength." *United States* v. *Visa*, 163 F. Supp.2d 322, 382 (2001). Schmalensee's testimony indicated that there were important scale economies at some size level—which limits the number of viable systems—but did not suggest that American Express or Discover were not at or close to the size at which additional scale economies would be marginal. Trial Testimony of Richard Schmalensee, *United States* v. *Visa*, 98 Civ. 7076 (BSJ), July 20, 2000, 5990–91. The court cited other testimony on this point. *United States* v. *Visa*, 163 F. Supp.2d 322, 389 (2001). The testimony cited did not, however, provide any evidence on whether American Express would currently gain any *significant* scale economies from additional volume.

other. It is also worth noting that Visa, with 47 percent of card volume to MasterCard's 26 percent, was much larger.[98] MasterCard would have been unable to compete effectively against Visa, as it certainly seemed to do, if Visa had enjoyed larger scale economies.

There was also no allegation by the government or finding by the court that American Express was unable to pursue product development or innovation initiatives because of a lack of access to Visa and MasterCard banks. For example, the "Blue" chip card that American Express touts as a significant innovation was developed without access to Visa and MasterCard issuers. Because it has neither a significant innovation nor a cost disadvantage, it is difficult to see how American Express is harmed as a system by the cooperatives' exclusivity rules.

The court's decision stated that "additional issuers leads to increased card issuance." It based this finding on general statements by industry executives that having more issuers is "always better."[99] Although this is generally true, it does not discuss "how much better" and whether that difference is competitively significant.[100] The court's finding was not based on or supported by any attempt by the government to quantify or otherwise assess the significance of any additional issuance on the American Express system. The government could have tried to estimate likely additional American Express volume from the elimination of the exclusivity rules. It could then have explained how such additional volume would have strengthened American Express as a system competitor. If it believed American Express would benefit from additional scale economies, that again is a subject that could be examined empirically. Without any of this evidence,

98. *United States* v. *Visa*, 163 F. Supp.2d 322, 341 (2001).

99. *United States* v. *Visa*, 387.

100. The court stated that "Visa U.S.A.'s general counsel testified that By-law 2.10(e) exists because of the likelihood that the number of American Express cards issued in its absence could be substantial" as supporting evidence for its belief that the impact was substantial. *United States* v. *Visa*, 387. In fact, Visa's general counsel testified that he did not have any view as to the likely number of American Express cards issued in the absence of bylaw 2.10(e), noting only that the possibility it might be substantially more than ten cards was one of the reasons for the rule. See Deposition Testimony of Paul Allen, *United States* v. *Visa*, 98 Civ. 7076 (BSJ), October 29, 1999, 360–62. Moreover, the number of cards issued by American Express bank partners that might be sufficient to disrupt the Visa system is different from the number of cards that might otherwise be considered competitively significant. For example, Schmalensee's testimony in the case suggested that disruption to Visa's corporate card program was possible and of significant concern to the association, even though its corporate cards accounted for only 2 percent of purchase volume on all Visa cards in the market defined by the court. See Direct Expert Testimony of Richard Schmalensee, *United States* v. *Visa*, 98 Civ. 7076 (BSJ), August 7, 2000, 109–12; *Nilson Report*, no. 689 (April 1999), p. 6.

it is not possible to say whether American Express has been significantly harmed by the cooperatives' exclusivity rules.

HARM TO COMPETITION. Because the trial court's decision does not assess the extent of harm to American Express, it falls short of providing a basis for assessing harm to competition or consumers. Here, following the court's finding of a network services market, the banks are viewed as the consumers in that market—they pay fees to the systems for the network services used by the banks in serving cardholders and merchants. The court did not address the matter of whether banks have been harmed by higher prices or lower quality for network services. Because Visa operates on a not-for-profit basis, its structure precludes setting system fees higher than costs, so that more (or less) competition would not lower (or raise) Visa's fees. The court's finding was based, in part, on the argument that four competitors must be better than two.[101] That presumption is typically made because prices with four competing for-profit competitors are generally likely to be lower than prices with two for-profit competitors. There could have been no concern in this case that Visa was using any market power to set supracompetitive system fees, nor did the government attempt to make any such claim, because Visa simply sets fees at cost.[102]

The government also presented no evidence that the cooperatives' exclusivity rules have allowed them to limit their own innovation or product development. In fact, the court found that the associations have "fostered rapid innovation in systems, product offerings and services. Technological innovations by the associations have reduced transaction authorization times to just a few seconds. Fraud rates have also decreased through a number of technological innovations."[103]

The court relied on its general finding that there would have been more volume on American Express in the absence of the exclusivity rules, which would in turn have led to greater competition in the network services market, which would have resulted in benefits to banks. But these

---

101. *United States* v. *Visa*, 163 F. Supp. 2d 322, 382 (2001).

102. In mergers of nonprofit hospitals the courts have recognized that the standard presumption that the anticompetitive accumulation of market power will lead to higher prices, which is also the incentive for firms to engage in such anticompetitive acts, is not present. That is, "by simply doing what is in their own economic best interest, certain nonprofit organizations ensure a competitive outcome, regardless of market structure." *Federal Trade Commission* v. *Freeman Hospital*, 911 F. Supp. 1213, 1222 (1995). See also *Federal Trade Commission* v. *Butterworth Health Corp.*, 946 F. Supp. 1285, 1296–97 (1996).

103. *United States* v. *Visa*, 163 F. Supp.2d 322, 334 (2001).

loose statements fail to assess competitive significance and could be made regardless of whether American Express would have had a 0.01 percent or 100 percent greater system volume in the absence of the exclusivity rules.

Missing in both the government's case and the court's decision was any serious attempt to assess the competitive significance of any additional card issuance. Contrast this to the evidence presented in *Mountain West*, in which Sears claimed that Visa's bylaw 2.06, prohibiting Sears from being a member of the Visa system, was anticompetitive.[104] Sears claimed that in the absence of Visa's bylaw 2.06 MountainWest (the Sears subsidiary seeking Visa membership) would have developed 13.9 million Visa accounts within seven years and that this would have benefited consumers.[105] Sears based this claim on its projections of the results of the proposed venture. Such quantitative analyses are commonly undertaken by large businesses before major decisions are made, and they can often shed light on *issues involving quantitative significance*. That American Express apparently did no projections of this sort before deciding to open its system to selected Visa and MasterCard members suggests that observers should be more skeptical of claims that substantial output would result from such agreements.

For the purposes of analyzing Visa's conduct, Richard Schmalensee in testimony in *Mountain West* accepted Sears's projections and found that even if the market did not grow, MountainWest's issuance would account for 1.4 percent of the market (stipulated to be general-purpose credit and charge cards) after two years and about 5 percent of the market after seven years. Considering this, Schmalensee concluded that adding another issuer of this size to an already highly competitive market would be unlikely to lower price or increase industry output significantly because the incremental issuer would mostly displace cards from existing issuers.[106] Since competition among issuers is intense and Visa and MasterCard are cooperatives that do not retain profits, there are no excess profits to be squeezed out of the business to benefit consumers. The Tenth Circuit Court accepted that analysis in reaching its conclusion in the *Mountain West* decision.[107]

---

104. *SCFC ILC, Inc.* v. *Visa U.S.A.*, 36 F.3d 958 (1994).

105. Direct Expert Testimony of Richard Schmalensee, *United States* v. *Visa*, 98 Civ. 7076 (BSJ), August 7, 2000, 68.

106. Trial Testimony of Richard Schmalensee, *SCFC ILC, Inc.* v. *Visa U.S.A.*, October 29, 1992, 2313–14.

107. *SCFC ILC, Inc.* v. *Visa U.S.A., Inc.*, 819 F. Supp. 956 (D. Utah, 1993), rev'd in part and aff'd in part, 36 F.3d 958, 971 (10th Cir. 1994), cert. denied, 115 S. Ct. 2600 (1995).

Dennis Carlton and Alan Frankel, economic consultants to Sears, disagreed with Schmalensee's analysis.[108] After the trial they published an analysis contending that entry by AT&T and GM had resulted in lower cardholder prices and that entry by MountainWest could have led to similar benefits for consumers.[109] Regardless of whether they were right on the merits, their analysis addressed the right issue—whether there was significant consumer harm.[110] Their analysis and Schmalensee's at trial in *MountainWest* were the types of evidence about which economists can engage in substantive debate. Without such analyses a court would have no meaningful economic basis for finding significant consumer harm.

Nothing approaching a 5 percent increase in card issuance or usage was demonstrated or alleged in *Visa*. The government at one point put forward a number of 8.8 million new cards, but that estimate was dismissed by an American Express witness as speculation, not projections.[111] The government's economic expert did not rely on these figures in his testimony and made no attempt to quantify the number of new cards that would be issued in the absence of bylaw 2.10(e).[112] Even taking this discredited number, however, the potential volume that would result from eliminating bylaw 2.10(e) is far less than Sears had projected from the elimination of bylaw 2.06 in *MountainWest* (8.8 million versus 13.9 million, a 58 percent difference, and a 1.7 percent share versus a 5 percent share, an almost 200 percent difference).[113]

At one point the government's economic expert, Michael Katz, considered a study of the experience of American Express alliances with Visa and MasterCard members in other countries (where similar exclusivity rules do not apply). This study would have used the international experience, with appropriate controls, to demonstrate consumer benefits from increased output or increased variety.[114] But it was not carried out or presented at trial.

108. Neither economist testified for Sears at trial. Sears relied on testimony from James Kearl.

109. Carlton and Frankel (1995). Neither this nor similar empirical analyses were presented by Sears at trial.

110. For an opposing point of view see Evans and Schmalensee (1999, pp. 257–62).

111. Trial Testimony of Stephen McCurdy, *United States* v. *Visa*, 98 Civ. 7076 (BSJ), June 20, 2000, 959–60.

112. Trial Testimony of Michael Katz, *United States* v. *Visa*, 98 Civ. 7076 (BSJ), July 12, 2000, 3728.

113. Katz did not attempt to quantify the impact on output or price of eliminating the exclusivity rules.

114. Trial Testimony of Michael Katz, *United States* v. *Visa*, 98 Civ. 7076 (BSJ), July 12, 2000, 3736–39.

Nor is it clear that there were any consumer benefits to be found from the international experience—card output from the American Express alliances with banks represented less than 1 percent of industry output in the relevant countries, and there was no evidence that any significant innovations came from those deals.[115]

LOST VARIETY. The second general finding by the court on consumer harm from the exclusivity rules was that consumers were deprived of choice and variety in card offerings, that some consumers might want an American Express card issued by a Visa member. Any exclusivity agreement, by definition, deprives consumers of choice and variety. Therefore any finding on consumer harm resulting from this lost choice and variety must include some assessment of the significance of these effects. For example, if an excluded manufacturer were unable to distribute its products effectively, depriving consumers of the ability to choose those products might constitute significant consumer harm. In this case the evidence indicated that American Express could reach all consumers.[116]

The court based its finding of consumer harm from lost variety on the following reasoning. It stated that "by working with American Express, banks could develop products that provide unique benefits to their customers." It cited the example of "Capital One and American Express in the United Kingdom, [where] it is undisputed that *either* Capital One or American Express could reach every consumer with an offer of *some* brand of credit card . . . yet, it is only the combination of Capital One and American Express that provides consumers the ability to take advantage of the combined skills of both entities."[117]

This argument proves too much. The same assertions could be made, for example, by virtually any manufacturer seeking distribution for its products by companies with some product differentiation. Every combination of manufacturer and distributor creates a product that is unique. Yet the courts do not automatically prohibit exclusive distribution agreements simply because the agreements, almost by definition, deprive consumers of products with "unique benefits." For example, United Airlines has an

---

115. Direct Testimony of Richard T. Rapp, *United States v. Visa*, 98 Civ. 7076 (BSJ), July 27, 2000, 50.

116. Trial Testimony of Kenneth Chenault, *United States v. Visa*, 98 Civ. 7076 (BSJ), June 29, 2000, 2438.

117. *United States v. Visa*, 163 F. Supp. 2d 322, 395 (2001).

agreement with Pepsi-Cola Company to serve Pepsi-owned soft drinks on its domestic and international flights. Consumers can no longer get Coca-Cola soft drinks on United flights.[118] Certainly there are consumers with distinct preferences for United flights and Coca-Cola. These consumers are denied the unique benefits of flying their preferred airline and drinking their preferred soft drink, but the courts, sensibly, do not prohibit such agreements—in part at least because few sensible people believe that the harm involved is significant.

The government did not attempt to demonstrate the importance of particular combinations of issuers and systems to consumers. Although there may have been marketing documents that promoted the benefits of certain issuer-system combinations, that does not resolve how significant these benefits are (or whether it would be possible for American Express or Discover to achieve these benefits without Visa and MasterCard issuers). The government could have asked its economic expert to examine how much consumers might value new issuer-system combinations or how much output might increase as a result of such offerings, but it apparently did not do so.

The actual decisions of industry participants indicate that these benefits may not be very great. For example, most major Visa and MasterCard issuers have chosen to dedicate themselves to one system or the other in recent years. If there were significant benefits from issuing both Visa and MasterCard in large quantities, it is unlikely members would have been willing to do this. Furthermore, for most of its history American Express has had no interest in using other banks as issuers. If there had been substantial benefits from additional combinations of issuers with the American Express system, the company would have sought much earlier to enter into such agreements. It is also worth noting that the court's findings included an extensive discussion of the many choices and features available to consumers.[119]

---

118. "United Airlines Will Start Serving Pepsi instead of Coke," *New York Times*, March 26, 2000, p. C4. Bork responds that the appropriate analogy is where there is an agreement by "United, American, Delta, Northwest, Continental, Southwest, and all the other airlines not to sell Coke or anything but Pepsi" (p. 64). Our main point here is simply that the loss of variety that the government called consumer harm is inherent to any type of exclusivity agreement. Bork's analysis again focuses on labels—that the associations' rules are agreements among competitors—rather than economic effects—could American Express effectively reach customers? He expressively disavows any need to address the economic question.

119. *United States* v. *Visa*, 163 F. Supp.2d 322, 395 (2001).

## Conclusions

There has always been a tension in antitrust cases over the risks of being so lenient that firms think they can get away with anticompetitive behavior and being so strict that the courts condemn practices that help consumers and thus stifle the very competitive process the antitrust laws seek to protect. There is no way to eliminate both risks; and the courts—and ultimately society—need to choose how to minimize the expected costs of the inevitable errors. At least in the context of predatory pricing, the Supreme Court has expressed a preference for erring on the side of acquitting the guilty rather than convicting the innocent. The *Brooke Group* test requires that plaintiffs meet a strong consumer harm standard, one that necessitates showing that over time predatory prices will reduce consumer welfare. Although the Court has not been quite so explicit about the consumer harm standard in other contexts, the logic of *Brooke Group* along with other decisions by the Court, especially *California Dental*, argues for a strong consumer standard in all rule-of-reason cases.

We agree with this approach. An error-cost analysis suggests that a strong standard of consumer harm would reduce the costs of making false convictions while, at least in the form we present, imposing relatively small costs from false acquittals. Most rule-of-reason cases involve complex factual situations. Practices are frequently challenged on the basis of economic theories whose predictions have not been empirically verified by the profession and whose assumptions are highly special and often untestable. There is nothing wrong with this: it is the best the economics profession can do. The only way for the courts to determine whether the challenged practices harm consumers is to seek relevant evidence. To paraphrase the Supreme Court in *California Dental*, one needs empirical analyses, not assumptions.

The Clinton administration disagreed with this approach. It invited the courts to rely on a weak standard for assessing liability in antitrust cases brought against Intel, Microsoft, and Visa and MasterCard. It was enough, it argued, to show that the practices challenged had harmed the competitive process through harm to competitors. And it suggested in some cases that there was no need to show, directly or indirectly (via significant harm to competition) that the challenged practices generally raised prices, lowered output, or reduced quality, thereby reducing consumer welfare. In the two cases that went to trial and for which there is a complete record—*Microsoft* and *Visa*—the district court accepted the government's approach.

In the one case—*Microsoft*—that has gone to an appeals court, the District of Columbia Circuit Court affirmed liability without reaching findings that the actions declared anticompetitive resulted in substantial harm to consumers or that there was a causal relationship between those actions and any significant changes in the competitive process that could lead to substantial consumer harm. And in *Visa* the district court found liability even though there was no evidence that the exclusivity rules at issue had resulted in significantly higher prices or lower output.

It remains to be seen whether other appellate courts and ultimately the Supreme Court will adopt what is, we believe, an unjustifiably toothless standard and whether this will, indeed, become the Clinton administration's lasting contribution to antitrust jurisprudence. It would be a sad day for consumers if the courts did so.

## References

Beckner, C. Frederick, III, and Steven C. Salop. 1999. "Decision Theory and Antitrust Rules." *Antitrust Law Journal* 67 (Winter): 41–76.

Bork, Robert H. 1978. *Antitrust Paradox: A Policy at War with Itself.* Free Press.

Carlton, Dennis W., and Allan S. Frankel. 1995. "Antitrust and Payment Technologies." *Federal Reserve Bank of St. Louis Review* 77 (December): 41–54.

Carlton, Dennis W., and Jeffrey M. Perloff. 2000. *Modern Industrial Organization,* 3d ed. Addison Wesley Longman.

Carlton, Dennis W., and Michael Waldman. 2002. "The Strategic Use of Tying to Preserve and Create Market Power in Evolving Industries." *Rand Journal of Economics* 33 (Summer): 194–220.

Chang, Howard H., and others. 1998. "Some Economic Principles for Guiding Antitrust Policy towards Joint Ventures." *Columbia Business Law Review,* no. 2: 223–329.

Crandall, Robert W., and Kenneth G. Elzinga. Forthcoming. "Injunctive Relief in Sherman Act Monopolization Cases." *Journal of Research in Law and Economics.*

Cusumano, Michael A., and David B.Yoffie. 2000. *Competing on Internet Time: Lessons from Netscape and Its Battle with Microsoft.* Touchstone Books.

Denger, Michael L., and John A. Herfort. 1994. "Predatory Pricing Claims after Brooke Group." *Antitrust Law Journal* 62 (Spring): 541–58.

Easterbrook, Frank H. 1984. "The Limits of Antitrust." *Texas Law Review* 63 (August): 1–40.

Evans, David S. 2001. "Dodging the Consumer Harm Inquiry: A Brief Survey of Recent Government Antitrust Cases." *St. John's Law Review* 75 (Fall): 545–59.

———. 2002. "Introduction." In *Microsoft, Antitrust and the New Economy: Selected Essays,* edited by David S. Evans. Kluwer.

Evans, David, and Richard Schmalensee. 1999. *Paying with Plastic: The Digital Revolution in Buying and Borrowing.* MIT Press.

Evans, David S., and others. 2000. *Did Microsoft Harm Consumers: Two Opposing Views.* AEI-Brookings Joint Center for Regulatory Studies.

Fox, Eleanor. 2002. "What Is Harm to Competition? Antitrust, Exclusionary Practices, and Anticompetitive Effect." *Antitrust Law Journal* 70, no. 2: 371–412.

Hahn, Robert W. and Anne Layne-Farrar. Forthcoming. "Federalism in Antitrust." *Harvard Journal of Law and Public Policy.*

Joffe, Robert D. 2001. "Antitrust Law and Proof of Consumer Injury." *St. John's Law Review* 75 (Fall): 615–32.

Houck, Stephen D. 2001. "Injury to Competition/Consumers in High Tech Cases." *St. John's Law Review* 75 (Fall): 593–614.

Hylton, Keith N., and Michael Salinger. 2001. "Tying Law and Policy: A Decision-Theoretic Approach." *Antitrust Law Journal* 69, no. 2: 469–526.

Litan, Robert E., and Carl Shapiro. 2002. "Antitrust Policy during the Clinton Administration." In *American Economic Policy in the 1990s*, edited by Jeffrey A. Frankel and Peter R. Orszag, 435–85.

Posner, Richard A. 1999. "An Economic Approach to the Laws of Evidence." *Stanford Law Review* 51 (July): 1477–1546.

———. 2001. *Antitrust Law*, 2d ed. University of Chicago Press.

Salop, Steven C., and Craig Romaine. 1999. "Preserving Monopoly: Economic Analysis, Legal Standards, and Microsoft." *George Mason Law Review* 7 (Spring): 617–71.

Whinston, Michael D. 1990. "Tying, Foreclosure, and Exclusion." *American Economic Review* 80 (September): 837–59.

———. 2001. "Exclusivity and Tying in *U.S.* v. *Microsoft*: What We Know and Don't Know." *Journal of Economic Perspectives* 15 (2): 63–80.

GEORGE L. PRIEST

5 | *Flawed Efforts to Apply Modern Antitrust Law to Network Industries*

The Antitrust Division of the Justice Department must, of course, continuously enforce the laws prohibiting price fixing, market division, and other cartel activities. These prosecutions may well represent the greatest benefit of antitrust enforcement to the American polity. Nevertheless, because of the continuity in enforcement, they appear routine, and no administration can claim particular credit for the results. Instead, to the extent any administration's antitrust policy establishes a distinguishing character, it is defined by the unusual cases that the Antitrust Division brings or those that become particularly prominent, often for reasons unrelated to either their economic significance or their contribution to the development of antitrust law.

In this respect the antitrust experience of the Clinton administration will be known foremost for its prosecution of antitrust claims against Microsoft, American Airlines and Visa and MasterCard. The *Microsoft* prosecution achieved extraordinary prominence because at the time the suit was filed Microsoft was the largest and most successful company in

I am grateful to the Program for Studies in Capitalism at Yale Law School and to Visa for support for this paper. I am also grateful to my colleague Michael E. Levine for illuminating discussions concerning airline networks and for comments on a draft of this chapter; to David Evans, Robert Hahn, Albert Nichols, Howard Chang, and Bernard Reddy for comments on a draft; and to Brodi Kemp and Tibor Nagy for research assistance. I have served as a consultant for two of the firms with litigation discussed in the text, Microsoft and Visa, though I was not involved in either litigation.

U.S. history. American Airlines, Visa, and MasterCard do not compare to Microsoft in market capitalization but remain highly significant entities, respectively, in the airline and credit payment industries.[1]

Prosecuting antitrust claims against prominent firms, however, does not automatically contribute either to the economy or to the law. Great cases may be bad cases and, as Oliver Wendell Holmes has taught us, great cases can make bad law.[2] Yet such a judgment of the antitrust enforcement of the Clinton administration is surely too harsh because, as shall be discussed later, these prosecutions have had little productive impact on the economy and hardly made law at all. The Clinton Justice Department lost its most important claims in *Microsoft* on appeal, lost *American Airlines* at district court and is likely to lose on appeal, and won one of its claims against *Visa/MasterCard* at district court, but on grounds that are largely unsupportable and are likely to be overturned on appeal.

There remains, however, a significance to these prosecutions and to the Clinton administration antitrust agenda because there is an underlying commonality to these cases: each was brought against a firm in a network industry. Although to my knowledge no officer responsible for the lawsuits has articulated exactly this ambition,[3] each of the prosecutions provided an opportunity to apply the antitrust laws to those industries that many regard to be the most significant for the new economy: network industries.

A network industry is different from a more typical hard goods industry such as those that manufacture cars or refrigerators. In a typical hard goods industry, one consumer's use of the good has little or no impact on the use by any other consumer. In contrast, in a network industry the interaction of consumers is important to the ultimate value provided by the industry, more particularly where the value of the product or service to consumers increases as the size of the network over some range increases. For example, Windows, the Microsoft operating system, along with the

---

1. Visa and MasterCard are associations rather than companies, as discussed later.

2. *Northern Securities Co.* v. *United States*, 193 U.S. 197, 24 S.Ct. 436, 48 L.Ed. 679 (1904).

3. Various Clinton antitrust officials discussed the application of antitrust laws to networks. Joel Klein, chief of the Antitrust Division, presented the theories of the *Microsoft* and *American Airlines* cases but did not suggest that they represented a connected approach toward networks Klein (2000). A. Douglas Melamed (1999), deputy chief of the Antitrust Division, argued that no different rules were necessary for network industries. There were two important discussions of network industries by Clinton administration economists, Shapiro (1996) and Rubinfeld (1998), but neither reviewed these cases in detail.

thousands of applications attending it, can be regarded as creating a network. A consumer using Windows gains greater benefits as there are more applications written for the system, and applications writers gain, and there are greater opportunities for new applications to be written, as there are more Windows users. More obviously, American Airlines operates a network of connecting routes and destinations. Travelers to or from those destinations benefit as the network expands or becomes more convenient; the destination markets and the airline benefit as the consumer base expands. Somewhat similarly, Visa and MasterCard have each created a network of banks offering credit and payment services connected to retail establishments that accept their cards. Consumers benefit as the network of establishments accepting each card expands; the establishments benefit as the number of cardholders increases.[4]

This description and understanding of the operation of network industries is uncontroversial. What is new is the application of antitrust doctrines to network industries in the modern era. There are earlier historical examples of networks: public utilities are essentially networks, as are railroads and telecommunications entities. In the premodern era the United States generally subjected industries of this nature to regulation on grounds that they were natural monopolies.[5] Although some regulation remains at local levels, direct regulation has been largely abandoned since the 1980s and is no longer seriously entertained as a mechanism for industrial control of the economy.

That leaves the antitrust laws. The principal significance of the Clinton administration's antitrust prosecutions, therefore, is that they represent the first systematic effort in the modern era to apply the antitrust laws to network industries.[6] The effort largely failed, and this chapter will discuss the sources of the failure. It is my view that the Antitrust Division during the Clinton administration possessed no coherent theory of the optimal organization of networks. The three prosecutions, themselves, were brought against networks of very different types and competitive structures. The

---

4. As will be explained later, there are also benefits from the expansion of this network to the banks that create it by issuing cards to consumers or signing up retail merchants to accept the cards.

5. See Kahn (1970).

6. There are, of course, many earlier antitrust cases addressing firms in network industries: for example, *United States* v. *Trans-Missouri Freight Assn.*, 166 U.S. 290, 17 S.Ct. 540, 41 L.Ed. 1007 (1897). More recently, the Justice Department brought suit against IBM and AT&T, although the network industry features of these industries played little role in the analysis. The department dropped the IBM prosecution and settled with AT&T, separating its regulated from its unregulated divisions.

division never developed a clear approach as to how the antitrust laws could improve the benefits to consumers provided by these networks. As a result, not only did the division generally lose the individual cases, it failed to provide guidance to courts to create legal doctrines or a method of legal analysis for the application of the antitrust laws to networks. That analysis remains to be developed.

In the first part of this chapter I review the three cases, explaining the division's claims and reviewing the outcomes of the litigation. I then analyze the competitive conditions in the respective networks and the Justice Department's theories of network competition. I conclude with a summary of the effects of the department's efforts.

## The Justice Department's Cases against Networks

This part briefly reviews the Justice Department's prosecutions of Microsoft, American Airlines, and Visa/MasterCard, attempting to explain the bases of the department's cases as well as the judicial treatment of these theories to date.[7]

### Microsoft

Microsoft created the dominant personal computer operating system in the world, Windows, possessing at the time of trial 95 percent of a market that the Justice Department defined as Intel-compatible personal computer operating systems.[8] The department (and eighteen states in concur-

7. Each of the cases remains in the courts. In *Microsoft* the district court has approved the company's settlement with the Justice Department and eight states, rejecting the challenge of nine separate litigating states. Subsequently, eight of the litigating states settled with Microsoft; Massachusetts continues to appeal the district court's ruling. The American Airlines and Visa/MasterCard cases are both on appeal from the respective district courts. Some further jurisprudence will surely result, though it is unlikely to directly address the network features of the industries in question, since that was not the Justice Department's focus.

8. There were issues in the case concerning the appropriate definition of the market, as there typically will be in network industry cases. This is an important matter in the application of antitrust law to networks, although largely beyond the scope of this chapter. But see text at nn. 36–37, 71–72, and nn. 39, 40, 45, 51, 69, 72. For the discussion of Microsoft's market share in the District of Columbia Circuit Court of Appeals' decision, see *United States* v. *Microsoft Corp.*, 253 F.3d 34, 51–58 (D.C. Circ. 2001).

rent actions)[9] claimed that this market share constituted a monopoly. The department did not, however, assert that Microsoft had acquired the monopoly illegally. Its theory instead was that the popularity and success of Windows had established over the years what the department called an "applications barrier to entry," protecting the monopoly from competitive entry. According to the government's theory, in the mid-1990s two potential competitors arose: Netscape's Navigator browser and Sun Micro-Systems' Java programming language and platform. These products posed competitive threats to the applications barrier to entry protecting Microsoft because both might evolve into platforms for running software applications without the need for Windows. According to the government, Microsoft recognized the potential threat and developed its own browser, Internet Explorer, to compete with Navigator and engaged in various practices to harm Java. By the time of trial Explorer had captured almost 50 percent of the browser market, largely at the expense of Navigator. Microsoft also had constrained Java's development by practices such as developing the Java Virtual Machine (JVM) with features unique to Windows, entering into agreements with internet service vendors to promote JVM exclusively, deceiving Java developers about the default settings for its Java development tools, and coercing Intel to stop aiding Sun.[10]

The Justice Department filed three counts against Microsoft that the district court found to constitute antitrust violations:

—violating section 2 of the Sherman Act (prohibiting monopolization) by illegally attempting to gain a monopoly of the browser market;

—further violating section 2 by engaging in various practices to maintain its operating system monopoly, chiefly promoting Internet Explorer to the detriment of Navigator and harming the other potential platform threat, Java; and

—violating section 1 of the act (prohibiting contracts in restraint of trade) by tying the sale of its browser to the sale of Windows.[11]

The tying claim was the most significant of the three counts because, if successful, it would have constrained Microsoft from adding further applications

9. Originally, twenty states and the District of Columbia joined the Justice Department's action. South Carolina dropped out during trial; New Mexico settled after the court of appeals' decision.

10. *United States* v. *Microsoft Corp.*, 253 F. 3d 74–78.

11. In addition to these counts the state plaintiffs had charged Microsoft with illegal leveraging, which the Court dismissed prior to trial, and illegal exclusive dealing, which the Court ruled was not supported by the evidence.

to subsequent versions of Windows to increase its popularity and entrench the applications barrier to entry.

The district court found in favor of the government on all three counts.[12] The Justice Department then requested, and the district court entered, an order breaking up Microsoft into a software applications company and a separate operating system company and imposing numerous restrictions on the operating system company.[13]

Upon appeal, however, the District of Columbia Circuit Court of Appeals largely reversed the district court's findings.[14] The court of appeals held that Microsoft had engaged in illegal practices to maintain its operating system monopoly, such as entering exclusive or restrictive licenses with original equipment manufacturers, internet access providers, and others as well as taking actions against Java. But it reversed the district court on all other counts. It overturned the conclusion that Microsoft had illegally attempted to monopolize the market for browsers. It also reversed the district court on the tying claim and, although it remanded the claim for a new trial, its discussion of the difficulties of applying the antitrust laws to a determination of the appropriate components of a product as complicated as an operating system was sufficiently skeptical that the Justice Department and the states dropped the tying claim.[15] The court of appeals also reversed and remanded the order breaking up Microsoft, again setting such a rigorous standard to justify the remedy that the department and the states announced they would no longer seek a breakup. Following the appeals court's decision the department and nine states entered a settlement with Microsoft, in essence enjoining the company from engaging in various practices, including those the court had found illegal.[16] Nine states refused to join the settlement and asked the district court for more extensive constraints on Microsoft and broader disclosure of Microsoft code. The court, however, upheld the reasonableness of the settlement and denied the litigating states' requests in their entirety.[17] Eight of the states

---

12. *United States* v. *Microsoft Corp.*, 87 F.Supp.2d 30 (D.D.C. 2000).

13. *United States* v. *Microsoft Corp.*, 97 F.Supp.2d 59, 64–65 (D.D.C. 2000).

14. *United States* v. *Microsoft Corp.*, 253 F.3d 34 (D.C. Cir. 2001).

15. The court of appeals was not convinced that the Justice Department had adequately supported definition of a separate market for browsers, greatly weakening the tying claim.

16. For a further discussion of the terms of the settlement, see Priest (2002).

17. *United States* v. *Microsoft Corp.*, 2002 WL 31439450, 2002-2 Trade Cases, para. 73,851 (D.D.C. Nov. 1, 2002); *New York* v. *Microsoft Corp.*, 224 F.Supp.2d 76, 2002-2 Trade Cases, para. 73,853 (D.D.C., Nov. 1, 2002).

have now settled with Microsoft (receiving attorneys' fees); Massachusetts has appealed the district court's ruling.

### American Airlines

The Clinton Justice Department next brought suit against American Airlines for its practice of reducing its fares to match those of low-cost airline entrants, outcompeting those entrants until they left the business, and raising fares thereafter. American was the only defendant in the case, but because all of the national airlines had engaged in similar practices, the prosecution was clearly intended to provide a precedent for a broader prohibition.

The case involved practices at Dallas–Fort Worth, a major hub for American, providing service to a large number of U.S. and foreign cities. During the mid-1990s several low-cost carriers entered the Dallas market offering flights to particular cities in competition with American. Vanguard offered service from Dallas to Kansas City, Wichita, and Phoenix; Western Pacific from Dallas to Colorado Springs; SunJet from Dallas to Long Beach—in each case at fares substantially lower than American's.[18] In each of these contexts and in others (the suit focused on seven destination markets from Dallas), once American saw that the particular low-cost carrier was successfully capturing some significant market share of travelers, it lowered its fare to match that of the competing carrier and sometimes increased frequency of service to retake the business. For each of these routes the low-cost carrier was forced to reduce frequency, ultimately ending service entirely. In many cases the carrier fell into bankruptcy. Uniformly, following the exit of the low-cost carrier, American raised its fares to the pre-competition level.[19]

The Justice Department pressed two claims: first, that this practice constituted predatory pricing in violation of section 2 of the Sherman Act; second, that American's success in driving out low-cost carriers on seven routes established a reputation that constrained entry by low-cost carriers on forty other routes. As framed by the department, the controlling issue was, under the predatory pricing standard established in *Brooke Group* v. *Brown & Williamson*, whether American had priced its service below an appropriate measure of cost and enjoyed a realistic prospect of recouping

18. *United States* v. *AMR Corp.*, 140 F.Supp. 2d 1141, 1146–51 (D.Kan. 2001).
19. *United States* v. *AMR Corp.*, 140 F.Supp. 2d 1155–68.

its losses by subsequent supracompetitive pricing.[20] In a summary judgment motion at the district court the issue was the relationship between American's price-matching fares and its costs of operation.

The controlling evidence for the motion consisted entirely of expert testimony on costs. Both the government and American relied on internal route cost and revenue metrics that the airline employed to evaluate route performance. American relied on a metric labeled VAUDNC (variable earnings plus upline/downline contribution net of costs). This metric provided an estimate of the revenue from the fare on a specific route net of operating costs (variable earnings) plus the additional revenue from the passengers' travel on upline or downline connecting routes net of those route costs. The airline showed that, for each route on which it matched the fares of the low-cost carriers, net earnings remained positive.

The Justice Department's expert, in opposition, evaluated route performance by four separate tests. Two measured incremental revenue following adoption of the competition-matching fare. They showed, not surprisingly, that American's incremental revenue on the competitive routes declined after it lowered its fares to match the competition. The court summarily rejected the appropriateness of the two tests.[21] The other two revenue tests asserted by the government were variations of American's metric FAUDNC (fully allocated earnings plus upline/downline contribution net of costs). These proposed measures differed from the airline's measure by including an allocation of costs of "aircraft ownership, fixed overhead, interest, equity and income taxes."[22] The Justice Department's measures thus resulted in a revenue number much lower than American's, obviously, because in a predatory pricing case, the government needs to show that the fare the defendant charged was lower than its costs of operation. By including an allocation of system or network costs, the metric showed that American had lost money on the routes after matching the low-cost carriers. The Justice Department claimed this was sufficient proof of predatory pricing.

The court rejected the department's argument and granted summary judgment for American. The court held that the airline had not engaged in below cost pricing, accepting American's metric that included variable but

---

20. *Brooke Group, Ltd.* v. *Brown & Williamson Tobacco Corporation*, 509 U.S. 209, 113 S.Ct. 2578, 125 L.Ed. 168 (1993). For the district court's statement and analysis of this standard, see *United States v. AMR Corp.*, 140 F.Supp. 2d 1195.

21. *United States* v. *AMR Corp.*, 140 F.Supp. 2d 1202–03.

22. *United States* v. *AMR Corp.*, 140 F.Supp. 2d 1174.

not fully allocated costs as showing positive net revenues from operating each of the routes. Important to the court was that "American's prices only matched, and never undercut, the fares of . . . low cost carriers on the four core routes. . . . American responded to, rather than initiated, non-promotional price reductions by low cost carriers." The government argued that the *Brooke Group* standard did not include a meeting-competition defense of this nature and that, even if such a defense were to be entertained, it was unavailable because "American not only reduced its fares, it increased the number of flights and therefore the number of seats available on the core routes."[23] The court, however, rejected the argument in its entirety, citing cases holding that a seller is not obliged by the law to "stand by watching its business being destroyed."[24] The court concluded that there were no significant strategic barriers to entry in the Dallas market and thus that recoupment of alleged predatory losses could not be achieved. It rejected the predatory threat theory as not supported by the facts.[25]

### Visa and MasterCard

Visa and MasterCard provide card payment services through a diverse set of banks and retail establishments in the United States and abroad. The Visa and MasterCard organizations, themselves, are not-for-profit associations that are each composed of thousands of member banks. The principal asset of these associations is the Visa or MasterCard brand name. The organizations are thus similar in some ways to franchisers who provide and promote a brand name.[26] Individual banks around the world may become members of the associations and be licensed to issue cards to customers and to acquire—sign up—retail establishments, which must promise to accept cards from customers of all banks in the association.[27] Each of these associations thus constitutes a large financial services network providing credit

23. *United States* v. *AMR Corp.*, 140 F.Supp. 2d 1204, 1207.

24. *United States* v. *AMR Corp.*, 140 F.Supp. 2d 1205, citing *Knuth* v. *Erie-Crawford Dairy Cooperative Association*, 326 F.Supp. 48, 52–53 (W.D.Pa. 1971).

25. *United States* v. *AMR Corp.*, 140 F.Supp. 2d 1209–15.

26. Visa and MasterCard also maintain and manage the card network and invest to improve its technological capacity. Their corporate structures are different from that of a typical franchiser because they are cooperatives, not companies independent of the franchisees.

27. Both the bank that issued the card to the consumer and the bank that acquired the retail account for the association earn fees calculated as a percentage of each retail transaction that is subtracted from the retail price remitted to the merchant. For a more detailed discussion of the compensation mechanisms of these associations, see text at notes 53–58.

and debit card service linking millions of individual consumers to millions of retail establishments.[28]

Visa and MasterCard possess a curious historical link. The earliest national credit cards were offered only by for-profit enterprises such as American Express, Diners Club, and Carte Blanche. During the 1970s the Visa and MasterCard associations grew by enlisting banks across the country as members. At the outset, membership was exclusive: Visa prohibited its members from becoming members of MasterCard, although it provided an exception for relatively small banks. After an inconclusive lawsuit by one of its members challenging the prohibition and with some pressure from the Justice Department, Visa relaxed the prohibition, allowing its members to also become issuing and acquiring members of MasterCard.[29] Despite the overlapping membership, it is widely accepted (and the court found) that Visa and MasterCard engage in serious and thorough competition against each other,[30] as well as against the principal proprietary card networks, American Express and Discover. Both Visa and MasterCard prohibit their members from issuing American Express or Discover cards.[31]

The Justice Department brought two claims against the associations. First, the department claimed that it was a violation of the antitrust laws for members of the board of directors (and other governing committees) of the respective associations to issue cards of the competing association. The department thus distinguished governance from card issuing. It admitted that "duality" in card issuance—a single bank issuing both Visa and MasterCard cards—increases competition. But the department claimed that governance duality—a Visa board member issuing MasterCards or the reverse—violated the antitrust laws. The department's second claim was that both Visa and MasterCard violated the antitrust laws by separately enforcing exclusivity rules that prohibited their respective members from issuing American Express and Discover cards.[32]

---

28. These features of the payment card industry are described in *United States v. Visa U.S.A., Inc.,* 163 F.Supp. 2d 322, 331–34 (S.D.N.Y. 2001). For an excellent historical and analytical discussion of the industry, see Evans and Schmalensee (1999).

29. *United States v. Visa USA, Inc.,* 163 F.Supp. 2d at 333–34, 345–46. MasterCard apparently did not impose a similar prohibition on its members with respect to Visa, though this is unimportant because of the Visa prohibition.

30. *United States v. Visa USA, Inc.,* 163 F. Supp. 2d at 332.

31. Diners Club and Carte Blanche are owned by Citibank, a large MasterCard and Visa member. Citibank's cards are exempted from the competitive card exclusivity prohibition.

32. There was no claim that the associations had agreed to enforce the exclusivity rules.

The district court rejected the department's claim with respect to governance duality, but held that the associations' exclusivity rules constituted a Sherman Act violation. With respect to dual governance the court held that the Justice Department had failed to demonstrate any competitive harm from the mere fact that a Visa or MasterCard board member issued the cards of the other association.[33] And although the government claimed there were various card innovations that had not been pursued because the members of the board of directors of each association were reluctant to improve one product at the expense of the other, the court held there was strong evidence suggesting that the proposed innovations had been abandoned for legitimate business reasons. The court also noted that there was a clear evolution in each association toward dedication by particular banks—often then chosen for board membership—to predominantly issue one of the cards alone.[34] This evolution effectively made the dual governance claim moot.

The court, however, held that the exclusivity rules prohibiting members from issuing American Express and Discover cards diminished competition. The Justice Department argued that the credit card networks should be analyzed as two separate markets: a market for general-purpose credit and charge cards, for which the relevant consumers were individuals using the cards and merchants accepting them, and a market for general-purpose credit and charge card network services.[35] The court found that there was ample competition in the market for general-purpose cards, but it found that the associations' exclusivity rules diminished competition in the market for general-purpose card network services.

The Justice Department's definition of the market for general-purpose card network services was important to the resolution of the case. According to the department, the member banks of Visa and MasterCard provide card network services through their efforts in brand promotion, antifraud services, and the like as well as in issuing cards to consumers and acquiring merchants to receive those cards. These services, although equivalent to services provided by American Express and Discover, are sufficiently distinctive to constitute a separate market.[36] By prohibiting member

---

33. *United States* v. *Visa USA, Inc.,* 163 F.Supp. 2d at 328.
34. *United States* v. *Visa USA, Inc.,* 163 F.Supp. 2d at 328–29.
35. *United States* v. *Visa USA, Inc.,* 163 F.Supp. 2d at 337–38.
36. *United States* v. *Visa USA, Inc.,* 163 F.Supp. 2d at 338–39.

banks from issuing American Express and Discover cards, Visa and MasterCard foreclosed American Express and Discover from taking advantage
of the issuing and acquiring services of the Visa and MasterCard member
banks. This foreclosure diminishes competition for network services. The
court accepted the proposition and enjoined Visa and MasterCard from
preventing their members from joining the American Express or Discover
networks.[37]

## Failings of the Department's Approach to Networks

The Justice Department largely lost the three cases it brought against
firms in network industries. It lost its most important tying claim against
Microsoft; it lost its predatory pricing claim against American Airlines
entirely; and it lost its dual-governance claim against Visa and MasterCard.
The department has, however, been successful so far (although the basis for
the holding is weak) in its exclusive dealing claim against Visa and Master-
Card. And, of course, it has achieved a settlement with Microsoft enjoining some of the company's more aggressive practices. But this "victory"
surely falls short of the department's ambition to restructure the operating
system market, either by breaking up Microsoft or by subjecting its further
development of Windows to judicial or department review had it won the
tying arrangement claim. Why has the department had so little success?

Note, first, that the prosecutions themselves and the theories on which
they were based appear quite disparate. In *Microsoft* the government
brought claims of attempted monopolization of the browser market, illegal
maintenance of its monopoly of the operating system market, and illegal
tying of its browser to its monopoly operating system, seeking finally to
break up the company. In *American Airlines* it claimed predatory pricing.
Finally, in *Visa/MasterCard* it claimed that the associations' governance
structures were illegal and that the associations had illegally imposed exclusive dealing requirements. These various claims do not appear to be linked.

Note also that these disparate claims bear no particular reference to
the network character of the industries or firms against which the claims
were brought. Across these cases, there is no coherent approach to the
application of the antitrust laws to networks. Worse, as I explain below,

---

37. *United States* v. *Visa USA, Inc.*, 163 F.Supp. 2d at 329–30, 407–09.

the department's approaches in these cases are inconsistent, even inconsistent internally within individual cases. In my judgment the Justice Department lost the cases because they were brought without any coherent or consistent theory about the operation of networks or the appropriate application of the antitrust laws to them. The department was unable to prove violations of the law because the practices it prosecuted generally served to increase competition and economic welfare in the respective network industries.

It is beyond the scope of this chapter to present a general explanation of the application of the antitrust laws to networks, but some guideposts might be helpful in evaluating the Justice Department's approach to the matter. Because in simple terms a network industry is one in which, over some large and relevant range, the benefit of the industry's product or service to consumers increases as the network expands, the most basic antitrust question must be what network configuration or operational characteristics best expand these benefits to consumers? This question resembles, but is not exactly equivalent to, an inquiry about achieving appropriate economies of scale. First, at the most general level the concept of the existence of network benefits implies continuously expanding scope as consumer benefits expand. Networks that meet this definition resemble natural monopolies, either because of expanding consumer benefits or because average production costs decline (the more common natural monopoly of the premodern era).[38]

Second, we know from experience that natural monopoly is not, or is not at certain points, the inevitable endpoint in network industries. Many industries comprise networks that compete partially or in their entirety. Indeed, two of the cases at issue involve industries with competing networks. The airline industry consists of a set of networks—the national airlines—that compete vigorously over high-volume routes but also separately dominate specific lower-volume routes. And the credit services industry shows substantial competition over card issuance and merchant acquisition. In addition, there is network-level competition between the four largely independent networks: the two nonprofit associations, Visa and MasterCard, and the proprietary networks, American Express and Discover. These examples suggest that network competition is possible in some industries because the benefits of expanding networks diminish over

38. For a discussion of network industries see White (1999).

some range or because of heterogeneous demand supporting competing networks, or because—as in the case of payment cards—it is nearly costless for consumers to participate in multiple networks. Nevertheless, there is no theoretical proposition that network competition can survive in every industry.

Beyond these simple points regarding industry structure, the question for antitrust application must be whether some particular practice increases network benefits. Practices that may appear anticompetitive in the context of multifirm industries or even anticompetitive when adopted by a monopolist may take on an entirely different cast where the objective is to expand consumer benefits by expanding networks. Again, the most direct standard must be how a given practice relates to the provision of network benefits to consumers. Regrettably, the Justice Department's theories in the three cases were innocent of these considerations.

### Attempting to Stimulate a Competing Operating System Network in Microsoft

Put in its best light, the Justice Department's theory in *Microsoft* sought to employ the antitrust laws to create the possibility for the development of a new operating system or platform to compete with the Windows network. The department believed that the Windows monopoly was protected by the so-called applications barrier to entry, which comprised the thousands of applications written for Windows but not for other operating systems. The department did not claim that Microsoft had acquired the Windows operating system monopoly or created the applications barrier to entry by illegal means. Rather, it saw Netscape's Navigator browser and Sun's Java as potential competitors to Windows because they might develop to establish alternative platforms for software applications. The department also saw Microsoft acting to protect its monopoly through the development of its own browser, its actions against Java, and through its continuous improvement of Windows. These actions both threatened the growth of the nascent Navigator and Java platforms and entrenched the applications barrier to entry. The department sought to employ the Sherman Act to constrain Microsoft and increase the possibilities of alternative platform growth in four ways:

—by enjoining Microsoft from engaging in practices that disadvantaged Navigator and Java (this was the monopoly maintenance count affirmed by the court of appeals);

—by penalizing Microsoft for its success in developing its competing browser, Explorer, which diminished Navigator's prospects (the attempted monopolization count, reversed on appeal);

—by forcing Microsoft to distribute Explorer separately from Windows (the tying arrangement count). A finding of an illegal tie and the necessity of separate sale would reduce Explorer's success in competition with Navigator and simultaneously provide the legal basis for judicial and administrative constraint on Microsoft's further improvement of Windows that might otherwise entrench the operating system monopoly (this count, too, was reversed on appeal); and finally,

—by breaking up Microsoft into separate operating system and applications companies (also reversed on appeal).

The difficulty with the Justice Department's theory and the reason it was successful in obtaining only very partial relief in its claims against Microsoft is that the department never developed, much less articulated, a coherent idea as to how a market with competing operating system networks would benefit consumers or why, if there were substantial benefits, competing operating system networks would not develop—as they had not developed—through market forces alone.

There was a central contradiction in the Justice Department's case. The department conceded that Microsoft had acquired its operating system monopoly on the merits. It brought no claims that Microsoft had monopolized the operating system market by any illegal acts. Nor did it claim that what it characterized as the applications barrier to entry was somehow created by artificially illegal means. Yet at the same time it sought to employ the antitrust laws aggressively to stimulate the development of a competing applications platform by limiting Microsoft's promotion of its browser, placing constraints on Microsoft's ability to add new features to Windows, and breaking Microsoft itself in two.

A theory of this nature is at heart contradictory and reflects an insufficient consideration of the benefits of the Windows operating system network. The department did not challenge that there were market reasons for the historical dominance of Windows. Greater competition among software operating systems, such as that between DOS and Apple's Macintosh or between Macintosh and earlier versions of Windows, had once existed.[39]

---

39. The department did successfully convince the court to define the relevant market as "Intel-compatible PC operating systems," chiefly Windows, which eliminated by definition the consideration of many competing operating systems. *United States v. Microsoft Corp.*, 253 F.3d 34, 51–54.

Over time, one operating system became dominant, at least for the vast majority of consumers. This dominance must reflect the vast network benefits from standardization of the operating system and the development of thousands of software applications dedicated to that system. Again, the Justice Department's failure or inability to attribute Microsoft's Windows monopoly to illegal acts or to some artificial interference in the market concedes the network benefits and, potentially, the expanding network benefits generated by Windows.

The department, however, sought to promote competition through the development of competing platforms such as the Navigator browser and Sun's Java. Yet it presented only the vaguest speculation—no doubt because that was all it could present—as to how a market with competing platforms for operating systems would operate.[40] As an abstraction, competition is preferable to monopoly, but the abstraction is only persuasive where the acquisition of a monopoly is artificial in some way. In the context of a network it is very difficult to measure or evaluate the scope of network benefits. Where a monopoly network has developed naturally—that is, without some artificial interference in market processes—the most plausible conclusion is that the monopoly derives from the extent of network benefits.

As a consequence the department's most basic theory consisted of little more than the pejorative characterization that the existence of thousands of software applications for Windows represented a harmful barrier to entry. But barring some artificial interference with market processes, the more plausible characterization is that these thousands of applications represent the benefits from creation of the network. By insisting that the existence of these benefits barred other firms from competing with Microsoft, the department put itself in the position of claiming that anything Microsoft did to improve the quality of Windows was an antitrust violation. Thus the department claimed that Microsoft's improvements to Explorer were a violation because they strengthened the applications bar-

---

40. There was basic confusion in the case with respect to the definition of the market that Microsoft was accused of monopolizing. The court of appeals accepted the Justice Department's claim that Microsoft had illegally maintained a monopoly in the market for operating systems that was protected by the applications barrier to entry. Applications, however, run on platforms, not necessarily on operating systems. Microsoft's illegal actions in the operating system market were said to inhibit the development of alternative platforms. There was no clear inquiry in the case as to Microsoft's position in the market for platforms, if such a market can be coherently defined.

rier to entry. But it turns antitrust law on its head to brand as a violation every investment to improve a product for consumers. And it is only rank speculation to assert that consumers of the monopoly network would benefit if there were one or more competing networks.

The Justice Department's speculative claims in this regard proved too weak to convince the court of appeals. The court did affirm that some of Microsoft's practices, such as its exclusive dealing contracts with personal computer manufacturers and others as well as its aggressive actions against Java, were violations because they did not constitute competition on the merits.[41] It rejected the rest of the counts because the department had not sufficiently thought through and justified the grounds for finding illegality.

Thus the court of appeals rejected the department's claim that Microsoft had illegally attempted to monopolize the browser market by concluding that its claims either were duplicative of the monopoly maintenance claims or were unsupportable because the department had not justified the existence of a separate browser market protected by barriers to entry.[42] Where the department claimed that Microsoft's expanding share of browser use showed an attempt to monopolize the browser market, the court was not convinced that a distinguishable browser market existed, revealing the inability of the department to provide a coherent or convincing conception of the market competition it hoped to stimulate.

Similarly the court, in the first instance, rejected the department's per se claim that it was illegal for Microsoft to incorporate (to tie) its Explorer browser into Windows on the grounds that it was impossible to know per se whether the improvement of a complicated product such as an operating system by the addition of new features did or did not benefit consumers.[43] The court's extended discussion of how the district court on remand should evaluate product improvements of this nature under the rule of reason[44] led the Justice Department and all eighteen states to drop the tying claim entirely. The court of appeals did not preclude the department from presenting additional evidence on this point if it wished to retry the claim. But the department and the states saw that the claim had no prospect of success because they were unable to articulate a conception of competing operating

41. For a further discussion of these features of the opinion see Priest (2002).
42. *United States* v. *Microsoft Corp.*, 253 F.3d at 80–84.
43. *United States* v. *Microsoft Corp.*, 253 F.3d at 89–94.
44. *United States* v. *Microsoft Corp.*, 253 F.3d at 95–97.

systems or platform networks in which it was at all plausible that consumers would benefit from a court or special master placing constraints on the improvement of the dominant operating system network.[45]

Finally, the court rejected the remedy breaking up Microsoft for exactly the same reasons. The Justice Department's break-up remedy was the most speculative feature of its entire case. What was the expected benefit from creating separate Microsoft operating system and applications companies? Was it believed that the applications company would develop its own new and competing operating system? Would the applications company pursue some other operating system, such as by aligning with the Navigator or Java platforms? Was the operating system company expected to develop competing applications? None of these questions was answered; indeed, they were not seriously addressed at the trial.[46]

The resolution of these issues left as the only successful claims of the department the illegality of various Microsoft practices, such as exclusive dealing contracts and its battle tactics against Java. No one has claimed that these practices were ever of great importance to Microsoft's business strategy or to the success of Windows or the Explorer browser.[47] They represent a "victory" for the Clinton Justice Department, but with no expected beneficial effect on the industry or the economy.[48]

In contrast, the government's focus on these practices in the abstract represents a great opportunity lost. The Justice Department's claims against the practices have no relation to their network context. Thus the resolution of the claims has added little to antitrust jurisprudence with respect to networks.[49] The court of appeals' analysis of the various practices does not

45. The court of appeals' decision also precluded the Justice Department from additional efforts to define a separate browser market, which further doomed the tying claim.

46. That the Justice Department allowed (encouraged?) the district court to enter the breakup order with only the most minimal hearing on these issues was hopelessly ill considered and ultimately fatal. See *United States* v. *Microsoft Corp.*, 253 F.3d at 101–03.

47. AOL/Netscape and Sun are separately pursuing private antitrust actions against Microsoft, necessarily making such claims. But the cases appear weak and are likely to be settled on modest terms.

48. Crandall (2002) has recently shown that the constraints imposed on Microsoft in the Justice Department settlement are extensive in comparison to remedies in other monopolization cases. However, there remain grounds for disagreement on how harmful the remedy will be to Microsoft's operations, which of course is an entirely different question from whether the remedy will provide any benefit to consumers or society. There is no societal benefit from simply harming Microsoft.

49. There are, perhaps, two exceptions. First, the court of appeals' discussion overturning the tying claim, explaining the difficulties of evaluating in an antitrust case what software components are socially appropriate, *United States* v. *Microsoft Corp.*, 253 F.3d, 84–97, is an important addition to tying arrangements jurisprudence, particularly because the most recent pronouncement by the Supreme

implicate their execution in the context of a network. According to the court, the practices—chiefly variations of exclusive dealing—are violations because they do not constitute competition on the merits,[50] a ruling equally applicable to any monopolist, network or not. It will be an interesting issue in some future case whether the law of exclusive dealing should be considered differently in a network context.[51] Again, if consumers benefit as networks expand, an exclusive dealing contract may serve to increase those benefits. This matter, however, and virtually all others, was lost in the department's failure to adequately consider and present the implications of the network character of the market for operating systems.

### Muddling Network Competition in Visa/MasterCard

*Visa/MasterCard* provides an interesting contrast to *Microsoft*. That case was brought against a company the Justice Department claimed possessed a network monopoly. The department sought to introduce competition into the industry by stimulating or protecting nascent potential networks that might compete with the dominant network. In *Visa/MasterCard*, in contrast, two claims were brought against associations in an industry in which there was substantial competition at both the issuer-acquirer and the general network levels. One of the department's claims—that it was anticompetitive for a member of the board of directors of one association to issue cards of the other—can be characterized as attempting to sharpen that competition, though the governance feature of the claim made any harm to competition remote and ultimately unpersuasive. But the second claim—that it was anticompetitive for Visa and MasterCard to restrict their members from issuing American Express and Discover cards—appears to embody the ambition of merging the competing networks over some range by compelling the Visa

---

Court on tying arrangements, *Jefferson Parish Hospital District No. 2* v. *Hyde*, 466 U.S. 2, 104 S.Ct. 1551, 80 L.Ed.2d 2 (1984), is quite dated. Less helpful, however, is the court of appeals' discussion and seeming acceptance of the Justice Department's characterization of the network benefits of Windows as constituting the so-called applications barrier to entry. Although the appeals court stated that it did not need to decide whether the thousands of Windows applications constituted a barrier to entry, it did endorse some version of the concept. *United States* v. *Microsoft Corp.*, 253 F.3d at 54–56. This holding, in an otherwise sharply intelligent opinion, is likely to contribute to confusion in the future understanding of network benefits.

50. *United States* v. *Microsoft Corp.*, 253 F.3d at 50, 52, 56, 59, 62.

51. *Microsoft* is not likely to be helpful toward this analysis because the litigation never made clear what market Navigator and Java were being excluded from. Neither was an operating system, and the court of appeals rejected the definition of a separate browser market.

and MasterCard associations to allow some of their members to also join the
American Express and Discover networks.

These two ambitions are internally inconsistent; the second claim is
inconsistent with the Department's ambitions in *Microsoft* to enhance
competition among separate networks. Worse, when carefully analyzed,
the Department's success (to date) in *Visa/MasterCard* is likely to diminish,
rather than increase, competition among the payment card networks.
These problems once again derive from an inadequate consideration of the
application of the antitrust laws to network industries.

It is helpful to understand competition in the payment card industry
in more detail. Visa and MasterCard are not-for-profit associations of
member banks. A bank may be a member of both associations and may
issue cards to consumers and acquire merchants to accept the cards.[52] The
separate Visa and MasterCard networks link these banks and their respective consumer and merchant clients together. In addition, American
Express and Discover are proprietary firms that manage networks that issue
cards and acquire merchants on their own. All four networks operate on
the basis of both cardholder fees and a small deduction from each retail
purchase, called the merchant discount. For Visa and MasterCard, part of
this discount is retained by the bank that acquired the merchant for the
network; the remainder (and larger part), called the interchange fee, is paid
to the bank that issued the card to the consumer. The issuing bank also
retains cardholder fees and finance charges. American Express and Discover, similarly, deduct a merchant discount from each retail transaction,
although they retain the discount (as well as cardholder fees) entirely themselves because, as single firms, they have both issued the card and signed up
the merchant.[53] Within the Visa and MasterCard networks the bank acquiring a merchant sets the merchant discount while the Visa and Master-
Card associations set interchange fees, which differ by type of merchant,
magnitude of the charge, and the like. Currently, the merchant discount in
the Visa and MasterCard systems averages about 2 percent; the interchange
fee averages about 1.4 percentage points of the 2 percent (again, to the

---

52. For more detail, see 163 F.Supp. 2d at 331–34; Evans and Schmalensee (1999).

53. The revenue bases of the bank associations and the proprietary companies differ significantly,
mainly because American Express operates mostly a payment card, rather than credit card, business.
Thus Visa and MasterCard member banks in aggregate obtain 78 percent of revenues from finance
charges, 12 percent from cardholder fees, and 10 percent from interchange fees. American Express ob-
tains 66 percent of revenues from the merchant discount, 19 percent from cardholder fees, and 15 percent from finance charges. Evans and Schmalensee (1999, pp. 164–65).

issuing bank), and the remaining 0.6 point is retained by the bank that acquired the merchant. Visa and MasterCard receive payments from their bank members sufficient to support coordinating the network, making technological improvements (such as accelerating card processing), and promoting the Visa and MasterCard trademarks.[54]

There are three forms of competition within the payment card industry. First, there is competition for consumers in direct card issuance, encouraging consumers to obtain a card, carry multiple cards, use one card rather than another, or shift credit balances to a new card.[55] Everyone is aware of this competition from the many credit and debit card solicitations most Americans receive by direct mail or in magazines offering cards with different (or no) annual fees, different credit limits, different interest rates, frequent flyer miles, and hundreds of other promotions.[56] Hence, there is competition among thousands of card issuers: within each association, as each bank encourages consumers to take its Visa or MasterCard card over that of another Visa or MasterCard member; between the associations, such as, say, a particular Visa card with one promotion versus a MasterCard with another; and against the two proprietary networks, American Express and Discover, which also seek to convince customers to take their cards.[57]

The second form of competition is in the acquisition of merchants to accept the cards. Here again the members of the associations compete against each other to acquire a particular merchant. American Express and Discover also seek merchants for their networks. There is competition over the magnitude of the merchant discount: in 1999 the American Express discount was 2.73 percent; Discover's, 1.5 percent; and Visa and Master-Card's on average, 2 percent.[58] Within the Visa and MasterCard associations, the magnitude of the merchant discount is importantly determined

---

54. *United States* v. *Visa USA, Inc.*, 163 F.Supp. 2d 332.

55. Evans and Schmalensee (1999, pp. 210, 219).

56. According to the court, Visa and MasterCard member banks mailed 2.9 billion card solicitations in 1999, equal to 2.4 solicitations a month to every American household. *United States* v. *Visa USA, Inc.*, 163 F.Supp. 2d at 334.

57. Evans and Schmalensee (1999) describe the different targeting strategies of the various networks. American Express for some time targeted higher-income consumers, in part because it chiefly offered payment cards rather than revolving credit accounts and derived most of its revenue from the merchant discount. Visa and MasterCard, in contrast, target consumers who are likely to maintain substantial credit balances but not approach insolvency, since these networks derive most of their revenue from interest charges on unpaid balances.

58. *United States* v. *Visa USA, Inc.*, 163 F.Supp.2d 333. In the early 1990s disgruntled retailers forced American Express to reduce its merchant discount. Evans and Schmalensee (1999, p. 76).

by the interchange fee. Thus the interchange fee is a competitive tool both between the associations—encouraging a bank to issue more Visa than MasterCard cards, for example—and as a determinant of the ultimate merchant discount. Merchant acquisition need not be exclusive: many merchants accept Visa, MasterCard, and American Express cards, although the networks could certainly seek exclusivity by making a sufficiently attractive offer to a merchant. As an example, the discount retailer Costco has entered a current agreement to accept only American Express credit and payment cards, and not those of Visa, MasterCard, or Discover.[59]

The third form of competition occurs among the networks themselves at the brand level, where each network separately promotes the benefits of its network to increase consumer and merchant acceptance as well as dedication by member banks. Current promotions such as "Some things are priceless. For everything else, there's MasterCard," or Visa's "It's everywhere you want to be," or its "and they don't take American Express" illustrate this network-level competition. Networks also compete technologically to facilitate claims processing both to consumer and merchant advantage.

In what ways did the Justice Department find the structure or practices of this industry anticompetitive? First, it claimed that it was a Sherman Act violation for the two associations to allow members of their respective boards of directors (or other governing committees) to issue cards of the other association. This is an odd claim on its face. The department did not argue that it was a violation for any single bank to be a member of both associations with authority to issue cards or to acquire merchants for both associations. Instead, it claimed that the antitrust laws are violated when those few banks that serve on one or the other board of directors issue cards of the competing association.

However unusual the claim, there is a glimmer of a theory here. The Justice Department appears to have been thinking that, although there was substantial competition between Visa and MasterCard as networks,[60] there might be even more competition if the members of the boards of directors were more seriously dedicated to their respective associations instead of allegedly being financially conflicted because they were members of both.

Some credit should be given to the department for considering means of increasing competition between networks in an industry that supports competing networks. The concept, however, is half-hearted, incomplete,

---

59. Costco formerly had an agreement to accept only Discover cards.
60. See text at nn. 55–59, and n. 64.

and inconsistent with the competitive realities of the industry. First, the department does not appear to have taken its governance theory seriously. It did not pursue a rigorous remedy: it did not seek to require board members to divest themselves of the other association's cardholders.[61] It only asked the court (in 2001) for an order requiring board members to shift their card holdings by 2003 so that 80 percent of the bank's total dollar volume from all cards was transacted on the network of which it was a director.[62]

Second, if the department were seriously committed to greater competition between the Visa and MasterCard networks, and at the same time believed that dual membership blunted competitive forces, it should have litigated whether dual membership should be prohibited in its entirety, requiring banks to choose between membership in either the Visa or the MasterCard network. An attempt of this nature, however, would have defied competitive reality.[63] Again, as is obvious from the multiple card solicitations we receive, card issuers compete strongly within associations and between the two associations, despite dual membership. Perhaps for this reason the department conceded that issuance duality—banks issuing both cards—enhanced, not reduced, competition at the consumer level, and it also conceded that Visa and MasterCard vigorously competed against each other.[64] These concessions greatly weakened the governance claim.

Finally (proof of the criticism), the department was unable to provide any convincing evidence to support its claim that dual governance was anticompetitive. The court stated that the department had failed to provide any credible examples of diminution in competition between Visa and Master-Card caused by their governing structure and further held that market forces were leading some governing banks to specialize in the cards of a single network, rendering the department's proposed remedy unnecessary.[65]

The Justice Department's second claim contended that it was an antitrust violation for Visa and MasterCard separately to prohibit their

61. The sale of entire card portfolios from one bank to another is a commonplace. Evans and Schmalensee (1999, p. 220).

62. During trial the government changed its request, adding a request for a prospective prohibition of dual issuance by board members. *United States* v. *Visa USA, Inc.,* 163 F.Supp. 2d at 328.

63. It would also have undercut the department's second claim, that it was anticompetitive for Visa and MasterCard to prohibit their members from issuing American Express or Discover cards.

64. The department seems to have conceded this point because the court explicitly found it to be so, without the need of discussion. See *United States* v. *Visa USA, Inc.,* 163 F.Supp. 2d at 332.

65. *United States* v. *Visa USA, Inc.,* 163 F.Supp. 2d at 328–29.

member banks from issuing cards of the competing proprietary networks, American Express and Discovery. As mentioned, the district court accepted the argument, a decision now on appeal. The department achieved success on this exclusivity claim, in my view, not on the merits of its antitrust analysis, but chiefly by convincing the court to accept its definition of markets in the payment card industry. The finding is unsupportable and is very likely to be overturned on appeal.

The department argued that the payment card industry consisted of two separate markets: first, a market for general credit and charge payment cards, that is, the market in which there was competition for consumers and merchants; and second, a separate market that the department labeled the market for "general-purpose credit and charge card network services."[66] This market comprises the competing networks themselves—the various banks and the two proprietary firms, American Express and Discover— that provide card issuance and merchant acquisition services. The government claimed, and the court accepted, that the member banks of Visa and MasterCard possess unique abilities in card issuance because of their relationships with their own depositors or their experience in issuing Visa and MasterCard cards, or both.[67] They possess equivalent expertise in merchant acquisition based upon their successful history.[68] Given this dual expertise, the Visa and MasterCard bylaws that prohibit member banks from issuing cards of the competing proprietary networks have the effect of foreclosing the market for issuance and acquisition services from American Express and Discover.[69]

However successful with the court, this is a highly peculiar proposition that cannot be defended as a matter of antitrust analysis. The proposition

66. *United States* v. *Visa USA, Inc.,* 163 F.Supp. 2d at 335.

67. Some of the largest members of Visa and MasterCard are "monoline" banks, firms with a bank charter but that exist to issue credit cards and do not accept traditional bank deposits. Evans and Schmalansee (1999, pp. 12–13).

68. *United States* v. *Visa USA, Inc.,* 163 F.Supp. 2d at 385–88.

69. *United States* v. *Visa USA, Inc.,* 163 F.Supp. 2d at 406–07. There was an additional confusion in the court's opinion concerning market definition. The court initially defined the market for network services as consisting of the contributions by the umbrella organizations, Visa and MasterCard, to their respective networks, such as brand promotion, transaction processing, and the like. *United States* v. *Visa USA, Inc.,* 163 F.Supp. 2d at 338–39. In its discussion of the violation, however, the network services that the court found foreclosed from American Express and Discover were the issuing and merchant acquisition activities of the individual member banks. *United States* v. *Visa USA, Inc.,* 163 F.Supp. 2d at 382–99. This is a significant confusion because Visa and MasterCard, as firms, do not themselves issue cards or acquire merchants; only their members do. No individual Visa or MasterCard member possesses market power in the issuance or acquisition market, totally undercutting the court's analysis.

possesses some superficial plausibility for two reasons: first, because Visa and MasterCard are associations of member banks, thus enabling the Justice Department to direct attention to the separateness of a member bank from the association itself; and second, because the court accepted a formulaic method of antitrust analysis unnecessary to the case. To see how the department exploited the organization of Visa and MasterCard as associations, imagine a slightly different corporate structure in the industry. Imagine that Visa and MasterCard were not associations of banks but were proprietary firms like American Express and Discover, where the banks were divisions or branch offices of the parent firm. This imagined change in corporate organization would have no effect on the analysis of competition among the four payment card systems at the network level.[70] But with this slight change in organizational form, the definition of the market accepted by the court and the claim of foreclosure become ridiculous. The market for "general-purpose card network services" comprises the competitors themselves. According to the Justice Department and the court, this "market" consists of the banks—the competitors of American Express and Discover—that possess expertise that American Express and Discover want to share. The basic claim of the department here is that Visa and MasterCard are foreclosing a market to American Express and Discover by not allowing those competing firms access to Visa and MasterCard assets or components. It is equivalent to a complaint by a manufacturer that it is foreclosed from a market because a competing manufacturer refuses to allow the complaining manufacturer to use the competing manufacturer's plant.

How did the court come to adopt such reasoning? It accepted the Justice Department's approach to antitrust analysis in rule-of-reason cases consisting of four separate steps: first, define the relevant markets; second, determine whether the defendant firms possess market power in those markets; third, determine whether the defendants restrain competition in the markets; and fourth, consider any procompetitive defenses. Thus the court accepted the department's definition of the two separate markets; secondly, it found that Visa and MasterCard possessed market power in both markets. Visa and MasterCard challenged the definition and the market power finding in the first market, that for general-purpose cards, arguing that the market should be defined to include checks, cash, and debit cards, which would have dramatically reduced the Visa and MasterCard market shares.

---

70. In this hypothetical, competition for consumers and merchants might be diminished if the parent firms restrained competition among their divisions, suggesting the advantages of the association form.

The court rejected their argument,[71] but the finding was unimportant since the court recognized the substantial competition for consumer card issuance despite the possession of market power. The defendant's objection to the definition of the market for card network services appears to have made no impression.[72] They could hardly have argued that they did not possess market power in that market; they were the market. The court then found restraint and dismissed the procompetitive defenses.

This four-step rule-of-reason analysis has become boilerplate, but it is totally unnecessary and ill designed for a case of this nature. Its adoption meant that the case was largely over once the department's definition of markets was accepted. At heart, the issue with respect to the exclusivity provisions related to competition among the four networks. The basic question was, will competition among these networks be greater or less if American Express and Discover are allowed to make deals with member banks of Visa and MasterCard to issue American Express and Discover cards? To analyze this question, there is no need for market definition or market power measurement.

In earlier days market definition and market power measurement were features only of merger cases. There the ultimate question always is whether the merger of two firms competing in the same market will increase market power and raise suspicions of oligopolistic pricing. Obviously, it is necessary for such an evaluation to define a relevant market and also necessary to measure market power because the decision to allow or disallow the merger is based on some intuition of the relationship between market power (relative size) and oligopolistic practices.

The market definition and market power measurement analyses were introduced into Sherman Act section 1 rule-of-reason cases not because it was necessary to the antitrust analysis of any practice at question, but as a prophylactic against unfounded judicial condemnation of procompetitive market practices. My teacher Ronald Coase used to remark that most of antitrust law had developed from economists and lawyers who, observing an industrial practice that they did not understand, concluded that it must be anticompetitive (this was before the 1980s). The contribution of the market definition and market power steps in rule-of-reason cases has been

---

71. *United States* v. *Visa USA, Inc.,* 163 F.Supp. 2d at 335–38.

72. Note the absence of discussion of a rebutting argument, *United States* v. *Visa USA, Inc.,* 163 F.Supp. 2d at 338–39. Here again, we see the court's confusion over the content of the market for network services, discussed earlier.

to dismiss claims when there is no demonstration that the defendant possesses market power—a helpful end, although achieved through very crude means. The ultimate question remains, how does the practice at issue affect competition?

In this case the claim that American Express and Discover have been foreclosed from a market for issuing cards and acquiring merchants is unsupportable. First, American Express and Discover perform their own card issuance and merchant acquisition activities. The court itself acknowledged that American Express was the largest card issuer in the country.[73] In addition, although the court makes no reference to this point, both the Visa member banks and American Express have in recent years contracted for merchant acquisition services from independent third parties.[74] Thus while it is surely true that the exclusivity rules deny American Express and Discover free access to member banks'—their competitors'—issuance and acquisition expertise, there is no plausible claim that the rules deny them access to issuance or acquisition services.

Second, there is no real foreclosure here in the sense of the existence of some artificial obstacle that prevents American Express and Discover from obtaining the services of banks that possess issuance or acquisition expertise. Even if one were to accept the dubious definition of a market consisting of the members of the competing associations, American Express and Discover are not denied access to them. Admittedly, once a bank enrolls as a member of Visa or MasterCard, access by American Express or Discover is denied. But there is no denial of access prior to the bank's enrolling as a member. Nor are American Express and Discover precluded from convincing a bank to leave the Visa or MasterCard networks to join the competing American Express or Discover networks.

In its discussion of the foreclosure claim, the court gave several examples of banks that had been approached by American Express or Discover, claimed that they desired to issue American Express or Discover cards, but

---

73. *United States* v. *Visa USA, Inc.,* 163 F.Supp. 2d at 333. The court ignored this point in its discussion of foreclosure. It is appropriate to compare American Express to the individual member banks rather than to the broader associations because it is the member banks that possess the issuance and acquisition expertise. The Justice Department and the court accepted the market power measurement of Visa and MasterCard in the aggregate, but the expertise that is alleged to have been denied is possessed at the individual bank level.

74. Evans and Schmalensee (1999, p. 134). Indeed, although the court does not address this fact, most third-party services acquire merchants for all the networks. Thus the finding of foreclosure of acquisition services becomes even less supportable.

declined once they appreciated that they would be terminated by Visa and MasterCard because of violation of the exclusivity rules. For example, the court found as evidence of foreclosure the refusal of Bank One to join the American Express network: "Bank One recognized . . . that any card-issuing arrangement with American Express would result in the unacceptably high cost of the bank losing its [Visa and MasterCard] association memberships."[75] But this is not an example of foreclosure as an antitrust violation; this is "foreclosure" because of competitive disadvantage. As between the offers of Visa and MasterCard and the offer of American Express, Bank One chose Visa and MasterCard. The rejection of American Express is the result of competition on the merits. It is antithetical to the basic purpose of antitrust law to claim that when an institution chooses to join one or another competing network, the networks rejected have been illegally foreclosed from that institution's services.

The exclusivity provisions in the Visa and MasterCard bylaws are in essence duty-of-loyalty provisions that compel a bank to be loyal to and to promote the network of which it is a member as long as it is taking advantage of the services of that network. Visa and MasterCard, as mentioned, are chiefly organizational shells that manage and promote their respective networks. In this respect they resemble franchisers, as organizations that develop and promote a franchise but do not provide the substantive services of the franchise themselves.[76] Duty-of-loyalty provisions are a commonplace in franchise contracts; indeed, they are ubiquitous. The Burger King hamburger franchise, for example, provides that during the term of the franchise the franchisee "may not own, operate or have any interest in any other hamburger business and may not own, operate or have any interest in any nationally or regionally branded fast food hamburger restaurant business."[77] Similarly, MAACO, the auto painting franchise, provides in its franchise contract, "You will devote your full time and energy to operation

---

75. *United States* v. *Visa USA, Inc.,* 163 F.Supp. 2d at 385. The court gives many other examples of the same point: "Advanta did not believe that it could simply leave both Visa and MasterCard in order to issue American Express cards"; "Although First USA would have liked to issue Discover cards itself, it would not do so for fear of losing the ability to issue Visa and MasterCard cards" (*United States* v. *Visa USA, Inc.,* 163 F.Supp. 2d at 384, 387).

76. They are different from franchisers, of course, because they manage the ongoing operations of the network and set interchange fees to maximize network success; see Evans (2002). They also invest heavily in improving the network's technological capacity and are cooperatives, not fully separate corporations.

77. Data obtained from FRANdata, NCB Franchise Services (a franchise contract collection agency), 2002, p. 7.

of the Center. You will not divert any business or customer of business to any competitor."[78] The Merle Norman Cosmetic franchise contract states, "You may not sell any merchandise that MNC has determined is inconsistent with the image of Merle Norman Studios or which may confuse the public as to its origin or quality or which will enable others to trade on the name or goodwill of MNC."[79] Indeed, of 150 franchise contracts available from a franchise contract collection agency, 142 contained duty-of-loyalty provisions of this nature.[80]

Duty-of-loyalty provisions appear to be adopted universally by firms in industries that are indisputably competitive, such as Wendy's, Taco Bell, and other fast-food franchisers as well as by those in highly diverse industries that cannot be imagined to possess market power of any magnitude, such as Curves for Women (fitness centers), Red, Hot and Blue Bar-B-Que, Wicks 'n' Sticks (gifts and crafts), Great Clips (hair care), Togo's Eatery (submarine sandwich shops), and Stanley Steemer (carpet cleaners).[81] This provides strong evidence that these provisions help increase franchise competition.

And there are intuitive reasons upon which to understand their economic function. Duty-of-loyalty provisions serve to align the incentives of the franchisee to those of other franchisees and more closely to those of the franchiser. All the parties must devote their energies to enhancing the attractiveness of the franchised product or service, and not those of competitors. They are particularly necessary in contexts—such as franchises or associations like Visa or MasterCard—where there is separate ownership of the firm that manages the trademark, the franchiser, from the franchisee firms that provide the product or service. Unlike a single firm with multiple branches, a franchiser cannot otherwise compel the independent franchisees to serve the ends of the larger franchise project. That is why such provisions are ubiquitous across highly diverse commercial contexts. Interestingly, but not surprisingly—a fact apparently unknown to the court—American Express's Travel Services franchise contract provides, "You may not belong to or associate with any organization or consortium which competes with AMEX's travel business or representative program."[82]

78. FRANdata, p. 1.
79. FRANdata, p. 6.
80. FRANdata, p. 6.
81. FRANdata, pp. 1–34.
82. FRANdata, p. 19.

There is no reason to think that the payment card industry is different in this respect. As in a typical franchise, the Visa and MasterCard member banks are independent of each other and independent of the Visa and MasterCard organizations themselves, except as individual members. For this reason, as in the franchise context, conflicted incentives are likely to arise in which one or another bank may act in a way that benefits itself to the detriment of the other member banks or the umbrella Visa and Master-Card organizations. The Visa and MasterCard loyalty restrictions restrain that form of conflict and align the member banks' incentives with those of both the other members and the larger organization. In this respect the provisions maximize competition with the proprietary networks, American Express and Discover.

It is an interesting question as to why, if these provisions enhance competition, Visa and MasterCard do not invoke them against each other; that is, why are banks allowed to become members of both associations? The answer is historical. At its origin, Visa did enforce a duty-of-loyalty clause prohibiting its members from joining the MasterCard network. One member challenged the prohibition; receiving no support from the Justice Department, Visa dropped the provision.[83] Duality in both issuance and governance followed and substantial competition between the associations continued. Whether the competition might still be strengthened if the associations were to become exclusive again is an interesting question, but it was not an issue that the Justice Department brought to the court.

The remedy that the department sought, however, was not to provide that every Visa and MasterCard bank could issue American Express and Discover cards. By the department's remedy, and the remedy adopted by the court, American Express and Discover may select which member banks they wish to associate with. This suggests exactly the problem that duty-of-loyalty provisions were designed to address: the prospect that American Express would select a bank or banks with which to affiliate to the exclusion of other member banks and to the harm both of those not affiliated and of the larger Visa and MasterCard organizations. The custom and expertise of a single Visa or MasterCard member bank are not the fruits simply of that bank's efforts, but also of the efforts of the entire network, including the other member banks and the larger organization. By allowing American Express or Discover to affiliate selectively, American Express

83. See text at note 29.

and Discover are given the opportunity of choosing to access those benefits without having invested to create them.

What was the Justice Department attempting to achieve? Again, the
department neglected the network context of the industry. Duty-of-loyalty
provisions increase cross-network competition: Visa and MasterCard versus American Express and Discover. That is why the district court's finding
that the provisions constitute illegal foreclosure is unlikely to be affirmed
on appeal. The holding stands upon a definition of the market and an
evaluation of the relative competitive benefits of loyalty restrictions that are
not supportable. Is it remotely plausible to conclude that all duty-of-loyalty
provisions in franchise contracts violate the Sherman Act? Can we imagine
Sherman Act prosecutions of Blimpie or Wicks 'n' Sticks or Red, Hot and
Blue Bar-B-Que because each asks its franchisees for brand loyalty?

### Ignoring Networks in American Airlines

In *American Airlines*, the third of the major cases the Clinton Justice
Department brought against companies in network industries, the department lost the case not because of an inadequate conception of network
competition nor because of a theory that was internally inconsistent, but
because it ignored the network character of the airline industry entirely.[84]
The department framed the case as involving nothing more than simple
predatory pricing: American had an established fare level; smaller carriers
entered to compete on various routes with substantially lower fares; American matched the fares; the entrants failed; American raised its fares thereafter; end of case. To the department, this practice was predatory; consumers were harmed by the return to higher fares and the threat that the
practice established that restrained low-cost carriers from entering to compete with American on other routes.

The weakness of the government's theory, however, was that pricing
behavior of that nature in a network industry such as airlines must be analyzed differently from standard predatory pricing. The government's theory
ignored entirely the existence of American's network of routes in contrast
to the limited routes between selected city pairs offered by the low-cost carriers. The failure to consider the network context of American's practices
led to the government's defeat in district court and its probable defeat on

---

84. *United States* v. *AMR Corp.*, 140 F.Supp.2d 1141 (D.Kan. 2001).

appeal. Indeed, when the context of price competition is considered between those airlines that operate networks and the low-cost carriers that do not, the case never should have been brought.

As in all predatory pricing cases, the government faced two evidentiary difficulties. First, it had to prove that, given a defendant's pricing practices, the revenues it earned were less than its costs of operation. Second, to establish a rational motive for the defendant to have accepted losses by pricing in this manner, it had to show that the predatory firm would be able to more than recoup those losses after the competing firms left the market.[85] The district court ruled that the government had failed to establish either point, rejecting the Justice Department's cost-and-revenue measure and finding no evidence to support the potential for recoupment. The department necessarily failed—the consequence of its neglect of the network character of the industry—because the difference between the government's and American's estimates of costs and revenue consisted entirely of American's costs of operating and maintaining its network.

Again, it is helpful to outline the nature of competition in the airline industry. Since the general deregulation of the airlines, much of the air traffic market in the United States has evolved into a hub-and-spoke system.[86] Various national airlines have established hubs at cities that generate substantial traffic or are otherwise centrally located. Traffic to or from the very largest cities—New York and Los Angeles, for example—is sufficient to support hubs of more than one airline. The hubs, then, provide service connecting a number of large and small cities through larger and smaller capacity spokes. The practical basis for the system is that, although there may be only a few passengers who wish to travel at any one time between any two cities at the ends of spokes, they can be joined at hubs with passengers from other spoke cities to support more frequent service to the smaller spoke cities. There is substantial competition among the national airlines at most of the spoke cities in their networks, although the level of competition among the nationals on routes providing links to smaller cities varies—one airline might offer frequent flights, another, much less frequent. Some of the smaller cities, however, accounting for a relatively small percentage of total traffic, are connected to only one or two hub networks. In addition to this network competition on routes with the traffic density

---

85. This is the controlling standard established in *Brooke Group, Ltd.* v. *Brown & Williamson Tobacco Corp.*, 509 U.S. 209, 113 S.Ct. 2578, 125 L.Ed. 168 (1993).

86. Conversations with Michael E. Levine have significantly increased my understanding of this industry. See also Levine (1987).

to support it, most of the national airlines also face fringe competition from low-cost, no-frills carriers that operate some flights on high-density routes and other flights between specific city pairs.[87]

The modern airline industry might thus be regarded as comprising competing airline networks plus competition in numerous denser markets from less-networked airlines. Each of the national airlines specializes in providing service over a specific set of cities, setting its hubs at those that generate the largest traffic or are best located for connections and then radiating its spokes to connecting cities to generate traffic for its broader system.[88] There is substantial competition among these networks on city-pair routes accounting for a large percentage of the total market where hub networks overlap. There is less competition on other routes important to maintaining the airline's network.[89] The low-cost carriers provide service on heavily traveled hub routes and otherwise attempt to specialize by offering service on carefully selected, but much restricted, city-pair routes.[90]

87. As an illustration of competition in the system, in October 2002 flight availability from the three New York airports (LaGuardia, Kennedy, and Newark) to Los Angeles was as follows. Three nationals dominated service: American offered 14 nonstop flights; United, 13; and Continental, 12. There was lesser service by other nationals: Delta offered 6 nonstop flights; Northwest, 1. Among low-cost carriers America West offered 3 nonstop flights; Spirit, 2; National, 2; TransStates, 1; and Trans Air, 1. From New York to the nearby Long Beach and Ontario airports, American offered 2 nonstop flights to Long Beach and 1 to Ontario; the low-cost carrier Jet Blue offered 6 flights to Long Beach and 1 to Ontario. In addition, Continental offered 3 nonstops from New York to Orange County; American, Delta, and United, 1 each. American also offered 40 connecting flights to Los Angeles through its hubs in Dallas and Chicago. Derived from *North American Executive Flight Guide*, October 2002, pp. 413–14, 451.

88. For example, in *American Airlines* the court found that in the third quarter of 2000, American offered nonstop service from its Dallas hub to 79 U.S. destinations with 467 daily flights and to 40 additional destinations with 237 daily flights through its commuter airline affiliate, American Eagle. *United States* v. *AMR Corp.*, 140 F.Supp. 2d at 1147. In October 2002 American flew nonstop to 82 U.S. cities, 19 cities in South America or the Caribbean, and 13 other international cities. Derived from *North American Executive Flight Guide*, October 2002, pp. 158–71.

89. As an illustration, a passenger wishing to fly from Portland, Maine, to St. Louis could obtain reasonably frequent (two to five departures a day) one-stop service on each of the six major airline networks through a variety of different connecting cites: on American through Boston, Chicago, Cincinnati, or New York; on Continental through Albany or New York; on Delta through Atlanta or Cincinnati; on Northwest through Detroit; on United through Chicago; and on US Air through Detroit, Philadelphia, Pittsburgh, or Washington. On the more heavily traveled segments, low-cost carriers provide segment competition. Thus Southwest offers service between Chicago, Detroit, and Washington to St. Louis. Derived from *North American Executive Flight Guide*, December 2002. This example was suggested by Michael E. Levine.

90. Southwest is a low-cost carrier but has established a major hub in Baltimore in some ways comparable to the hubs of the nationals. For example, Southwest does not incur costs to facilitate passenger connections; passengers can make low-price connections, but much less conveniently than through those provided by the network airlines. I would characterize Southwest as a quasi-network carrier.

The government brought two claims against American: first, that the airline's practice of matching the fares of the low-cost carriers and increasing capacity on seven routes was predatory, and second, that matching fares on the seven routes established a reputation that had thwarted the entry of low-cost carriers on forty other routes. The case was resolved at summary judgment. Both the Justice Department and American submitted expert reports making opposite claims about the relationship between costs and revenues on the seven routes. The Justice Department, using an internal American metric, FAUDNC (fully allocated earnings plus upline/downline contribution net of costs), claimed that American's fare-matching revenues net of costs were negative on these routes. American claimed that an alternative cost metric, VAUDNC (variable earnings plus upline/downline contribution net of costs), was the appropriate measure; it showed profits for each of the routes.[91] The case, therefore, turned on whether the government's cost metric or American's was the better means of evaluating whether American's pricing was predatory.

According to the court, the principal difference between the two measures was that the government's metric included an allocation of network costs:

> the overhead or general operating expenses incurred in running an airline, particularly one with a hub-and-spoke network, that are not driven . . . by operating or not operating a particular flight or route. Examples of such expenses at American include dispatch, city ticket offices, certain station expenses, a portion of pilot pay and other labor costs, certain maintenance expenses, American's flight academy, flight simulator maintenance, investments in yield management and other computerized systems, and sales and advertising.[92]

The court accepted that the standard for evaluating whether a firm's prices are predatory is whether they are below average variable costs; it found American's revenue metric, rather than the government's, to more closely approximate the variable-cost standard. The court also held that the means by which American competed with the low-cost carriers should not be penalized, emphasizing that American had only matched, not undercut, the lower fares. Although the government also complained that American had increased capacity on these routes, the court was incredulous

---

91. *United States* v. *AMR Corp.*, 140 F.Supp. 2d at 1202–03.
92. *United States* v. *AMR Corp.*, 140 F.Supp. 2d at 1176.

that increasing capacity should be regarded as an antitrust violation. It dismissed the government's theory of competitive threat summarily.[93]

What to make of the Justice Department's case? American's practice of matching the fares of low-cost carriers until they leave the market bears some semblance to classic predatory pricing. The resemblance disappears, however, when the network context of the industry is considered. Like many other networks, an airline network requires both considerable initial investment and continuing investments and operating expenditures common to the network to maintain it. These costs cannot be specifically attributed to provision of service on any particular route. Airline networks face two forms of capacity constraints. At the lowest level, when a plane is committed to a particular route at a particular time, the airline has strong incentives to fill the plane's seats: any empty seat represents a loss of some marginal revenue.[94] This constraint explains the plethora of promotional fares, especially last-minute fares, now available on the Internet. The second capacity constraint relates to operation of the network as a whole. The airline will want to define its network so that over the long run it generates enough aggregate travel to support the entire system. Thus it must determine to which cities to extend spokes and the number and size of flights along those spokes that will generate that traffic.

The airline must include in its aggregate fare structure some allocation of common network costs in addition, of course, to the incremental costs of operating flights on each spoke. Because passengers with many different itineraries are accommodated on each spoke flight, even most of the incremental costs cannot strictly be attributed to any specific city-pair route. These common network costs were included in the government's FAUDNC metric, which incorporated 97–98 percent of American's total costs; they were not included in American's VAUDNC metric, which incorporated only 72 percent of total costs. The court presented another description of this difference. The FAUDNC metric included "fixed expenses for American's maintenance facilities . . . including rent, computer systems, communications and utilities . . . [and] exterior cleaning." In addition,

93. *United States* v. *AMR Corp.*, 140 F.Supp. 2d at 1207, 1215–18.
94. Obviously, the carrier can adjust the size of planes that it commits to a route and the number of flights per day, subject to the network capacity concern discussed later. Once the airline has committed the flight, however, it has every incentive to price aggressively to fill the plane.

American's system-related overhead expenses consist of a wide range of activities required to operate a large hub-and-spoke airline. These include management, supervision and administrative expenses associated with aircraft load and clearance . . . as well as flight attendant staffing. In addition, this category includes functions such as headquarters marketing and sales, capacity planning, corporate communications, pricing and yield management, flight operations and safety, cabin design and crew scheduling. Passenger advertising is also part of this category.[95]

The court believed that American allocated these common network costs arbitrarily across routes.[96] But this is highly unlikely. One would imagine that American's fare determinations would represent some effort to approximate competition-restrained, Ramsey-like pricing with the network component of costs allocated in a way to minimize aggregate decline in demand.[97]

American's pricing practices in response to the low-cost carriers must therefore be seen in a different light. American responded to lower fares of its low-cost competitors by shifting its recovery of common network costs to routes on which it was not constrained from recovering costs because of low-cost carriers' competition. It did so to maintain a sufficient passenger volume and contribution to common costs to sustain its broader network. As mentioned, the court found that, putting aside these general network costs, American's net revenues on the competitive routes remained positive.[98] After the low-cost carriers left the market, American reallocated the previous share of general network costs to the previously competitive routes.

There are several inferences to be drawn from this history for evaluating effects on social welfare. First, the chief difference between American's precompetition fares and the fares of the low-cost carriers seems to be the general network costs faced by American but not faced by the carriers that do not provide a network.[99] American's network provides consumer value, however, because at equivalent fares, consumers chose to fly on its network

95. *United States* v. *AMR Corp.*, 140 F.Supp. 2d at 1174, 1176–77.
96. *United States* v. *AMR Corp.*, 140 F.Supp. 2d at 1176.
97. For an interesting discussion of this problem and of the general welfare effects of the allocation of joint costs in a complex service system, see Levine (2002).
98. *United States* v. *AMR Corp.*, 140 F.Supp. 2d at 1175.
99. Michael E. Levine has informed me that the low-cost carriers have much lower labor costs because of the absence of a history of unionization. Thus American must be achieving other efficiencies in operation to be able to match their fares and remain profitable.

rather than stay with the low cost-carriers, which went out of business. This history also suggests that before American's fare reduction the low-cost carriers were essentially free-riding on American's network. Their customers were taking advantage of the low fares the carriers offered on some of the spokes of American's network but were then using the American network for the rest of their trips. At equivalent fares these customers preferred to concentrate their travel on the network airlines that could satisfy more of their travel needs. Otherwise, the customers would have been indifferent as between American and the low-cost carriers after American lowered its fares. Low-cost fares between city pairs can only survive in competition with a network if there is sufficient city-pair travel unrelated to access to the network. American's increase in capacity was, just as the court found, a response to increased traffic at lower fares and was not additionally predatory. That American raised fares again after the low-cost carriers failed represents only a reallocation of general network costs to those routes, a reallocation totally appropriate because the existence of the network benefits all routes in the system.

The court emphasized that American had only matched, not undercut, the low-cost carriers' fares. If there are consumer benefits from fare reductions to maintain a network, is there any reason to limit those reductions to only matching the lower fares as opposed to undercutting them? If one were totally certain of positive benefits from the existence of the network, undercutting prices would force the low-cost carriers out of the market faster, and so might be beneficial.[100] A legal rule that constrains the network firm to only matching fares, however, may be useful in establishing a market test of the value of the network to consumers. At equal fares, passengers shifted from the low-cost carriers to American in sufficient volume to drive the low-cost carriers out of the market. This shift, again, demonstrates the existence of benefits to consumers from the American network. If American had undercut the fares of the low-cost carriers, the pure network benefit would not have been as evident.

Again, by ignoring the network context of American's practices, the Justice Department misdiagnosed the consumer welfare effects of the Dallas fare wars entirely. The misdiagnosis led the department to positions that were hopelessly impractical. While certainly true as a matter of doctrine that there is meeting-competition defense in section 2 case law, a

---

100. This point resembles the policy of prohibiting entry in regulated networks.

meeting-competition defense is supported by common sense. As the court asked, isn't it natural to expect a firm facing a new competitor to meet its price? The government's competitive threat count was equally impractical. It is difficult to see what was added to the case by contending that American's allegedly illegal practices on Dallas routes constituted a threat that restrained entry on other routes. If the department had been successful in proving illegality with respect to the Dallas practices, American would be forced to stop them. Any future threat would disappear. It would seem that the only ambition of the department's theory of competitive threat was to provide a private cause of action for low-cost carriers who had never entered in competition with American, hardly a defensible governmental objective.

## The Clinton Justice Department's Network Record

The prosecution of the three cases against network firms by the Clinton Justice Department, of course, required the investment of substantial governmental resources and entailed substantial defenses. That there are few positive results to be shown for the effort is regrettable. The failings derive from an inadequate consideration by the department of the practical benefits from the operation of the respective networks.

In *Microsoft* the Justice Department faced a operating system network that it conceded had attained the status of a monopoly naturally, not on the basis of artificial restraints. Despite the clear implication that the monopoly resulted from the broad network benefits of standardization, the department sought to restructure the industry to stimulate the development of competing platforms. In *Visa/MasterCard* the department faced an industry characterized by vigorous competition among four networks and, even further, among thousands of banks within two of them. Contrary to its ambition in *Microsoft*, the department sought to break down the divisions between the competing networks to allow American Express and Discover to merge at their election into the Visa and MasterCard networks.[101] Finally, in *American Airlines* the Justice Department seemingly disregarded the network context of the airline industry entirely, to its own ill, since the grounds on which the court dismissed its claims were based on the need for American to incur costs to sustain its network.

101. The department's governance claim in *Visa/MasterCard* was insignificant.

Over the past decade a considerable literature on the economics of network industries has developed.[102] Much of this writing, however, has focused on the most novel of network topics, such as tipping, first-mover effects, lock-in, and the like. These subjects are of substantial academic interest, but they are essentially esoteric and do not address the practical understanding of how networks are organized and how they operate. To date the literature on network industries in both economics and law has failed to develop practical grounds for understanding what legal interventions will serve to enhance network benefits for consumers.[103]

The three cases brought against network firms by the Clinton Justice Department have not significantly advanced that understanding. Indeed, I believe that the department's ambitions in each case were counterproductive. In *Microsoft* the department sought remedies that would restructure the industry to impose some form of competition in a context that appears to be a natural operating system monopoly. In *Visa/MasterCard* its remedy would have diminished network competition either by merging American Express in part into the Visa and MasterCard networks or by allowing American Express and Discover to pick off portions of the associations' networks to their own advantage. Finally, in *American Airlines* the department's remedy—preventing American from reallocating network costs to sustain the network—would ultimately lead to erosion of the network.

Although these efforts have been generally thwarted by the courts, at this writing one of the litigating states is seeking on appeal more serious constraints on Microsoft than the mild conduct remedies imposed in the Justice Department settlement.[104] And the court order allowing the selective merger of American Express with Visa and MasterCard has yet to be reversed on appeal. The grounds on which the respective courts stopped the department's misguided prosecutions, regrettably, were not a firm understanding of the operation of networks, but a combination of intuition and judicial caution. The District of Columbia Circuit Court of Appeals in *Microsoft* intuited that it was difficult for a court to know how to configure an information product such as an operating system and warned of the dangers of condemning product design though tying doctrines. With admirable

---

102. See, for instance, Katz and Shapiro (1994); Economides (1996).
103. For a helpful beginning toward this goal see White (1999).
104. Though, in my opinion, with little chance of success.

judicial restraint it compelled the Justice Department to prove consumer benefit before seeking an order to break up Microsoft. Faced with those challenges—challenges it should have addressed before bringing the prosecution—the department dropped the claims. Similarly, the district court in *American Airlines* intuited that American's pricing behavior in matching the fares of the low-cost carriers must relate to its support of its network and dismissed the department's claims. The court in *Visa/MasterCard*, in contrast, perhaps distracted by an unhelpful market definition, ignored the intuitions that would follow from observation of high competition in the payment card industry. Again, I expect that ruling to be overturned.

The Clinton Justice Department's failures in these cases and the limited contribution the cases make to an antitrust jurisprudence dealing with networks expose the need to evaluate the operation of network industries more carefully. If America's new economy is to be dominated by networks, we will need a much firmer understanding than currently exists as to how the antitrust laws can be employed to increase network benefits to consumers.

# References

Crandall, Robert W. 2002. "The Proposed *Microsoft* Decree and Past Antitrust Remedies: A Systematic Comparison." Critical Legal Issues 112. Washington: Washington Legal Foundation (November).

Economides, Nicholas. 1996. "The Economics of Networks." *International Journal of Industrial Organization* 14: 673–699.

Evans, David S. 2002. "The Antitrust Economics of Two-Sided Markets." Publication 02-13. AEI-Brookings Joint Center for Regulatory Studies (September).

Evans, David, and Richard Schmalensee. 1999. *Paying with Plastic: The Digital Revolution in Buying and Borrowing.* MIT Press.

Kahn, Alfred E. 1970. *The Economics of Regulation.* John Wiley.

Katz, Michael L., and Carl Shapiro. 1994. "Systems Competition and Network Effects." *Journal of Economic Perspectives* 8: 93–115.

Klein, Joel. 2000. "Rethinking Antitrust Policies for the New Economy." Speech presented at the Haas/Berkeley New Economy Forum. Portola Valley, Calif., May 9.

Levine, Michael E. 1987. "Airline Competition in Deregulated Markets: Theory, Firm Strategy and Public Policy." *Yale Journal of Regulation* 4: 393–494.

———. 2002. "Price Discrimination without Market Power." *Yale Journal of Regulation* 19: 1–36.

Melamed, A. Douglas. 1999. "Network Industries and Antitrust." *Harvard Journal of Law and Public Policy* 23: 147–157.

Priest, George L. 2002. "U.S. v. Microsoft: A Legal and Economic Analysis of the Settlement." Contemporary Legal Notes 41. Washington: Washington Legal Foundation (March).

Rubinfeld, Daniel L. 1998. "Competition, Innovation, and Antitrust Enforcement in Dynamic Network Industries." Speech presented to the Spring Symposium of the Software Publishers Association. San Jose, Calif., March 24.

Shapiro, Carl. 1996. "Antitrust in Network Industries." Speech presented at the American Law Institute and Amercan Bar Association conference on Antitrust/Intellectual Property Claims in High Technology Markets. San Francisco, January 25.

White, Lawrence J. 1999. "U.S. Public Policy toward Network Industries." AEI-Brookings Joint Center for Regulatory Studies (December).

# Contributors

**Robert Bork**
American Enterprise Institute

**Howard H. Chang**
NERA Economic Consulting

**David S. Evans**
NERA Economic Consulting

**Robert W. Hahn**
American Enterprise Institute

**George L. Priest**
Yale Law School

**Richard Schmalensee**
Massachusetts Institute of
Technology

**Lawrence J. White**
New York University

# Index

Advertising, 77

Airline Deregulation Act of *1978*, 25

Airline industry: competition in, 148–49; consumer issues, 66; deregulation, 3, 11n2, 25, 64–65, 69; exclusive dealing agreements, 63–64; fares and fare matching, 151; hub-and-spokes structure, 25, 64–66, 148–49, 152; mergers, 11n2; networks, 3, 5, 9, 25, 129, 147, 149, 151, 153; predation, 25. *See also* American Airlines; *United States v. AMR Corp.*

Allchin, James, 50

Aluminum producers, 37

American Airlines: competitive companies, 27, 47, 123, 152; consumer effects, 153; fares and costs, 152, 153; hubs, 64–65, 66; as a network, 151–53; predatory practices, 9, 27, 64, 66, 123, 123–25, 153. *See also* Airlines; *United States v. AMR Corp. et al.*

American Enterprise Institute–Brookings Joint Center for Regulatory Studies, 1–2

American Express: banks and, 63, 104, 143–44, 146–47; as competitor to Visa and MasterCard, 5, 9, 56–57, 103, 104,
126, 127, 137, 142; consumer use of, 57, 58; data collection by, 58; debit and multichip cards, 58; exclusivity, 138, 145–46; fees and earnings, 136; harm to, 7, 105, 106–13, 128, 140, 141, 143; market power, 140–44; as a network operator, 119; as a proprietary system, 102, 106, 136, 141; purchase of bankcard portfolios, 107; size of, 106, 112, 118; Travel Services, 145–46. *See also* Discover Card; Payment and credit card systems; *United States v. Visa USA, Inc., et al.*; Visa/MasterCard

America OnLine. *See* AOL

Andreessen, Marc, 100

Antitrust litigation: of the Clinton administration, 118, 154–56; effects of, 118; error-cost analysis, 83–91; settlement of, 20–21, 89, 91; tensions of, 114; use of economics in, 12, 88, 89. *See also* Clinton (Bill) administration; specific cases

*Antitrust Paradox, The: A Policy at War with Itself* (Bork), 54

Antitrust policies, in general: *Brooke Group* test, 76–78; Clinton standard for, 6, 8, 73, 75, 79–80, 84; duality and

# JOINT CENTER

AEI-BROOKINGS JOINT CENTER FOR REGULATORY STUDIES